6/99

D0937031

WITHDRAWN

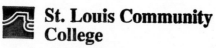

St. Louis Community College

Forest Park
Florissant Valley
Meramec

Instructional Resources
St. Louis, Missouri

GUYANA: MICROCOSM OF SUSTAINABLE DEVELOPMENT CHALLENGES

St. Louis Community College
at Meramec
Library

This book is dedicated to my children, Jade and Karl,
and to my wife Pauline.

Guyana: Microcosm of Sustainable Development Challenges

BARRY MUNSLOW
University of Liverpool

Ashgate

Aldershot • Brookfield USA • Singapore • Sydney

© Barry Munslow 1998

All rights reserved. No part of this publication may be reproduced, stored in a
retrieval system, or transmitted in any form or by any means, electronic,
mechanical, photocopying, recording or otherwise without the prior permission
of the publisher.

Published by
Ashgate Publishing Ltd
Gower House
Croft Road
Aldershot
Hants GU11 3HR
England

Ashgate Publishing Company
Old Post Road
Brookfield
Vermont 05036
USA

British Library Cataloguing in Publication Data
Munslow, Barry
   Guyana : microcosm of sustainable development challenges
   1.Sustainable development - Guyana 2.Sustainable
   development - Government policy - Guyana
   I. Title
   333.7'09881

Library of Congress Catalog Card Number: 97-77537

ISBN 1 85972 642 9

Printed and bound by Athenaeum Press, Ltd.,
Gateshead, Tyne & Wear.

Contents

Acknowledgements

This book could not have been produced were it not for the tremendous kindness and generosity of the Guyanese people, professionals in very many spheres, who gave of their time in interviews or made their research data or findings available. Whilst it is unfair on all the others who contributed so much I would like to single out for special mention Patrick Williams, Thomas Gittens, Walter Chin and Bridget Bouell, who all helped enormously.

The United Nations Environment Programme working with the United Nations Development Programme country office in Georgetown were totally supportive when I worked with them as a policy and institution building advisor at the beginning of the 1990s. The current work, needless to say, with all of its shortcomings, does not reflect any official position and the errors are solely mine.

It is with regret that I confess to not having had the opportunity to spend time with the new government in discussing so many of the issues raised in this book. But I hope they will view this as a positive contribution to their policy reflections on these important topics. The opportunity may arise in the future to continue the debates.

Other specialists who have shared their abundant knowledge of the country with me include Mark Pelling, a young scholar of great promise at Liverpool University, Colin Henfrey, Mike Gilman, Audrey Coulson, the organisers and participants at the splendid conference on Environment and Development in Guyana held in the Department of Geography, Royal Holloway, University of London in May 1997. A very special final word of thanks goes to Marian Hoffmann, a good friend of the environment, who so painstakingly typed and helped produce the final manuscript and to Debbie Paddison who did so well with reorganising the layout.

Acronyms

APA	Amerindian Peoples Association
CDC	Community Development Council
CIDA	Canadian International Development Agency
CITES	Convention on International Trade in Endangered Species of Wild Fauna and Flora
DTL	Demerara Timbers Ltd
EAC	Environment Advisory Council
EIA	Environmental Impact Assessment
EIS	Environmental Impact Study
EIU	Economist Intelligence Unit
EPA	Environment Protection Agency
EU	European Union
FAO	Food and Agricultural Organisation
GAHEF	Guyana Agency for Health Sciences, Education, Environment and Food Policy
GEMCO	Guyana Environmental Monitoring and Conservation Organisation
GDP	Gross Domestic Product
GFC	Guyana Forestry Commission
GGMC	Guyana Geology and Mines Commission
GNRA	Guyana Natural Resources Agency
GOG	Government of Guyana
GRSP	Guyana Rainforest Sustainability Programme
GUYWA	Guyana Water Authority
IAST	Institute of Applied Science and Technology
IMF	International Monetary Fund
IPM	Integrated Pest Management
IUCN	World Conservation Union

MAFP	Ministry/Agency Focal Point
MMA/ADA	Mahaica-Majaicony-Abary Agricultural Development Authority
NARI	National Agricultural Research Institute
NCLDO	National Congress of Local Democratic Organisations
NDC	Neighbourhood Democratic Council
NDIIA	National Democratic Institute for International Affairs
NEMP	National Environment Management Programme
NGO	Non Governmental Organisation
NPC	National Parks Commission
ODA	Overseas Development Administration (UK)
OECD	Organisation of Economic Cooperation and Development
PNC	People's National Congress
PPP	People's Progressive Party
PSTF	Programme for Sustainable Tropical Forestry
PWC&RD	Ministry of Public Works, Communication and Regional Development
RDC	Regional Democratic Council
SD	Sustainable Development
SIMAP	Social Impact Amelioration Programme
STAP	Short Term Action Programme
TEV	Total Economic Value
TSA	Timber Sales Agreement
UDG	United Dutch Group
UG	University of Guyana
UNCED	United Nations Conference on Environment and Development
UNDP	United Nations Development Programme
UNEP	United Nations Environment Programme
US	United States
WPA	Working People's Alliance
WWF	Worldwide Fund for Nature

1 Guyana's challenge

Guyana's experience in the wider picture

Guyana as a case study has much to offer to illuminate some of the central challenges facing the World in the area of environment and development. For a start, Guyana belongs both to Latin America and to the Caribbean. Whilst its social, cultural and political orientation may be overwhelming towards the English speaking Caribbean, it is physically located on the Latin American mainland and its natural resource base has more in common with Brazil and Venezuela than Trinidad and the British Virgin Islands. With the people and the politicians hugging the coastline and looking out towards the Caribbean as their primary point of reference, it is perhaps little wonder that effective management of the vast natural resource base of the interior has been neglected.

Within the boundaries of this relatively small country some of the most critical sustainable development challenges facing the planet are to be found. Two stand out in relation to the natural resource base. Firstly, the complex issues surrounding the conservation and sustainable management of the tropical forest. Guyana contains a pristine section of the rapidly diminishing Amazonian tropical rain forest. As a result of economic stagnation and opposition to foreign capital during its radical socialist phase, exploitation of the forest resources of the country was restricted.

The Guyanese case is particularly instructive as it offers the relatively novel possibility in recent times of developing an effective management of a rich natural resource base that has not already been devastated or at the very least badly damaged. Most of Guyana is still vibrant Amazonian rain forest. Roads, logging and mining which have wreaked destruction on large areas of its giant neighbour, Brazil, have had a limited impact as yet. It is not yet beyond redemption. Yet with the liberalisation of the economy, powerful mining and logging interests are dramatically expanding their area of operations and it is essential to create an appropriate framework for the sustainable management of the forest resource. There is still time for effective management strategies to be put in place.

What is and is not being done and what lessons can be learnt? Guyana provides some clues. It is unique amongst the Caribbean countries in having an abundant natural resource base. Yet to date it has often failed to maximise the development opportunities in an effective manner.

1

A second area of global concern involves the vexed issue of coastal zone management. Guyana is one of the most threatened countries of all in relation to global warming and a potential rise in sea levels. The Guyanese situation is critical as nearly all of the population live right along the coastal strip and are dependent upon an elaborate system of sea defences and drainage channels. This area is subject to regular floods and devastation. Coastal sea defences were subjected to a long period of neglect and a sizeable investment is now required to restore the situation.

Guyana provides a very interesting case study for a whole number of reasons, not only in relation to critical natural resource management issues, although these will remain our central focus. It is more widely instructive for the broader comparative development experience on two accounts. It is a country which experimented for a considerable period of time with a radical socialist development model. It now shares the experience of going through a transition from state centred autocratic socialism towards becoming a free market oriented democracy along with the countries of Eastern Europe, Angola, Mozambique, Ethiopia, Laos, Cambodia, Vietnam and a number of other former socialist states. It may indeed provide some pointers for a post-Castro era in Cuba. There is much to learn in both a positive and a negative sense from its particular experience. In addition, and providing an even broader comparative dimension, is its experience of undergoing structural adjustment and democratisation, a set of circumstances shared with a great many states in the South.

If we take these latter two comparative dimensions together then what is the interest in the Guyana case study for the more general body of knowledge? Looking back over a forty year post-independence experience from a perspective at the end of the 20th century, Guyana's cooperative socialism proved no more successful as a radical alternative development model than other variants on the same theme tried elsewhere. Indeed, it led the country into stagnation, bankruptcy, corruption and autocratic rule.

The turn around towards a new strategic direction has taken a long time. It began when President Hoyte replaced Burnham in the mid-1980s and accelerated with the first free elections held for a very long time in 1992 when President Jagan came to power. The democratic elections helped propel the structural adjustment agenda forward and there has been a constant period of economic growth ever since, throughout the 1990s. Yet there were groups in society who suffered considerably with the policy changeover and it would be wrong to ignore these costs. But evidence suggests that overall, the effects of both transformations offer positive long term prospects, certainly compared with the development *cul-de-sac* of past policies. Will Guyana provide a qualified success as a transition model? This is not in any way to minimise the hardship and suffering of those who have borne the brunt of the costs of such a

2

monumental transition. Overcoming poverty still remains the central challenge. Yet is there sufficient evidence now both globally and specifically in relation to Guyana to suggest that the move to private enterprise offers a positive way forward?

One has to enter all of the normal caveats concerning potential comparabilities. Guyana, unlike so many other socialist countries, did not experience extensive and devastating destabilisation and civil wars. Guyana also never propounded a hardline Marxist-Leninist ideology, nor did it formally establish a one party state. Yet the ruling party manipulated the electoral process to guarantee one party rule for almost three decades. Moving from a sham to a genuine set of democratic elections marked a mighty turn-around from past practices. Its economic policies whilst emphasising cooperatives in the rhetoric, effectively involved nationalisations controlled centrally by the state. The problems of unpackaging a bureaucratic, indebted and inefficient centrally controlled economy were therefore very similar.

Guyana offers some hope that the new approaches may serve the country better. These policies are bringing economic growth, albeit at some early cost to the poorer sections of society.

A note of caution is required, however, in the post-Cold War political era of revived ethno-nationalist conflicts worldwide. The politicisation of ethnicity in Guyana is all too tangible. The winners and the losers of the new policy dispensation in the short term at least, reinforce ethnic fault lines. There is a danger that a growing underclass of Afro-Guyanese losers in the current policy and political climate will provide a breeding ground for increasing criminality, drug dealing and social unrest. The possible costs associated with the new development policy pathway is a broader issue posing a serious challenge worldwide. South Africa is looking down the barrel of the same gun. Whilst everything may be done to create an economic climate conducive to inward investment, the free market to flourish and so forth, leaving an impoverished underclass to ignite soaring and increasingly violent crime will have absolutely the opposite effect to that which the favourable macroeconomic policy climate is intended to generate. Crime and violence puts off inward investors and increasingly complicates the life of budding domestic entrepreneurs, unless as in Russia say, the criminals and entrepreneurs work together. The challenge facing Guyana into the 21st century is to prevent potential intra-ethnic conflict and to keep the lid on criminality. Some sharing of the benefits of economic growth is required if the current winners are not to create a climate which will ultimately undermine their aspirations and achievements.

A final observation of the more general lessons to be learnt from Guyana concerns the limitations of many of the theoretical lenses used to guide the research and policy thinking in the country in the past.

Guyana has been the recipient of various theories employed to explain a reality which singularly failed to comply with the precepts of the theories and failed to offer a viable alternative development agenda. Without being in any way definitive we can point to the overwhelming predominance of dependency theory, varieties of marxist, socialist and black power thinking which completely determined the spectrum of debate from the mid-1960s to the late 1980s. In retrospect, it is clear to most observers that these contributed to the developmental *cul de sac* into which the country fell.[1] The gender spectacles provide a further example. Alissa Trotz captures the dilemmas in this literature quite well in her paper which: "argues that analyses of patriarchy which prioritise gender at the expense of other social constructs through which women's experiences are refracted, are ultimately unable to offer an explanatory framework which can adequately account for the production of similarities and differences among women".[2] Trotz's work demonstrates that the accepted notion that the household itself is a critical determinant in female labour supply is belied by the experience of Afro-Guyanese women, where it does not necessarily have any explanatory credentials. Hence Trotz warns clearly of the limitations of academic overemphasis on gender as an explanatory factor at the expense of other social relations.

In addition to the intrinsic interest of Guyana as a case study of a country facing the challenge of sustainable development, there are, in sum, broader lessons to be learnt for the comparative experience. Guyana is almost uniquely placed as a crossroads of currents in the South. The population comprises immigrants from Africa, India, China, Portugal and Britain as well as the indigenous Amerindians. Guyana is physically located in South America but its population primarily relates to the Caribbean community. The great global issues of tropical forest and coastal zone management are at the forefront of Guyana's sustainable development challenges. These issues are being faced in the wider context of a profound transition from socialist central state planning to free market economics through a structural adjustment and democratisation programme.

The challenges

Guyana is physically located in the north-east corner of the South American continent yet in the cultural perception of the majority of its peoples it is a part of the Caribbean island community. Both economically and socially there are family and friendship ties to North America and Great Britain also where so many Guyanese live and work. This has profound implications for the degree of environmental sensitivity of the majority of the population who live on the coast and who never venture into the vast forested interior where the only means of access is by foot, boat, hiring expensive light aircraft or taking the tortuous journey by lorry along the few poor roads that exist. Guyana borders on three neighbouring territories, but has no proper road connection to any of these. Guyana has poor international as well as internal transport and communications networks. It is most definitely a backwater.

The peoples of Guyana have travelled long and far. The original inhabitants, the Amerindians, originated in Asia. Centuries ago they migrated across to Alaska, down through North America, eventually to inhabit the dense forests of Amazonia. They are now only a tiny minority of the total population. The next significant human wave of immigrants came involuntarily. They were brought in as slaves from the African continent by European traders and settlers, to provide labour for the plantations. These are the Afro-Guyanese. They were followed by indentured labour from India, and this group, the Indo-Guyanese, came to make up the largest population group in the country. Chinese, Portuguese and British came and stayed as well, as influential minorities. The post-independence politics of the country as they have developed reflect these broad ethnic divides.

The British colony of Guyana was granted internal self-government in 1961 and the radical, predominantly Indo-Guyanese People's Progressive Party (PPP) of Dr Cheddi Jagan was elected into office. This was perceived as a threat to Western interests in the region who successfully contrived to bring into power what was assumed at the time to be the more pro-Western, predominantly Afro-Guyanese People's National Congress (PNC) of Forbes Burnham in 1964 in alliance with the small business oriented, United Force Party which mobilised the Amerindian electorate. In 1966 Guyana became fully independent and four years later was declared a republic.

The PNC contrived to rig the political system in such a way that they retained power for almost three decades even though the Afro-Guyanese were a minority compared with the Indo-Guyanese. Yet to the great chagrin of the Western powers, the PNC underwent a radicalisation and in October 1980 declared the world's first Cooperative Republic. In reality the main cooperative to benefit was the PNC cabinet, according to its critics. Soviet influence increased and Western aid and investment declined. The low point was achieved in 1985 when Guyana was expelled from the IMF.

The management of the natural resource base of the country in the post-independence PNC Burnham era was based upon an avowed socialist ideology, built upon the twin concepts of nationalisation of the natural resources accompanied by a verbal commitment to cooperatives. In reality, this meant a growing authoritarian one party supremacy over government institutions and an ever greater dominance in controlling the economy.

Burnham consolidated his rule by adopting a radical ideological agenda which stole the clothes of the opposition at a time when Marxism and black power were in the ascendancy in the 1970s, and he consolidated that power by building up the security forces, a task made easier by neighbouring countries adventurism at the beginning of that decade. Military expenditure grew almost fourfold from 3.2% of GDP in 1970 to 12.4% by 1986. More money spent on arms meant less resources for development.

The process of economic nationalisation proceeded fairly rapidly and by the late 1970s only one fifth of GDP lay outside of state control. Our key concern is to review what was the impact of the nationalisation on the management of the natural resource base. We will review its impact sector by sector in the book and the challenges facing the country in moving away from this complex historical legacy.

Guyana serves as an object lesson of the affect of a socialist development strategy in a poor country on the periphery of the global economic system. Its failure to develop the natural resource base proved to be a *de facto* environment conservation strategy. The result of this radical socialist historical developmental *cul de sac* creates both opportunities and constraints. The opportunities involve the chance to avoid the pitfalls of a rapid free-for-all pillaging of the resource base in order to actually guarantee a more sustainable usage. This is possible because the resource base was left relatively in tact through neglect and the absence of investment. The constraints centre on the temptation to cash in on the neglect of investment in the past and create a free-for-all in which social and environmental concerns receive nothing more than perfunctory appraisal, or become a further opportunity for rent-seeking activity by the state.

Guyana faces a formidable development challenge possessing the second lowest GNP per capita in the Western hemisphere after Haiti, $310 in 1989. It is the poorest country in Latin America. That development challenge is inevitably at the forefront of everyone's minds as people try to improve their day to day lives.

This country of under 800,000 people had amassed a debt of almost $2 billion by 1990, which represented approximately $2,500 for every citizen, over eight times the per capita GNP. According to the World Bank's World Debt tables, the following year the total external debt rose to over ten times the GNP. The economic decline began in 1976 and worsened considerably over the 1980s. GDP fell a dramatic 16% in 1982-83, stagnated in the mid-1980s and dropped more than 10% in the late 1980s.

6

The period of economic decline was undeniably associated with the socialist experiment undertaken at that time. In the light of this domestic experience, a changing global economic climate and increasing international pressures and following the death of Burnham in 1985, the stage was set for change. With Hoyte assuming the presidency, in the following year the government slowly began to change policy by encouraging foreign investment and the private sector. In 1988 an Economic Recovery Programme was announced in a proposed agreement with the IMF. But the IMF initially held back on funding to test the government's commitment to the reforms. Divestment of the nationalised bauxite and sugar industries was set in train along with other areas of state ownership. An IMF monitoring agreement in April 1989 opened up a process of debt re-scheduling and the resumption of external capital inflows. In July 1990 a formal IMF stand-by and enhanced structural adjustments were finally agreed. The process of decline was halted and GDP grew by 6.1% in 1991 and by 7.7% in 1992. Full Western support remained dependent on the holding of free elections. After many delays these did eventually take place in October 1992, and the old government was removed from power. Dr Cheddi Jagan and the PPP took office and proceeded to consolidate the dramatic swing away from the old centralised state dominant model towards a market based policy.

To revive the ailing economy, new investment is required and a revitalisation of all the basic infrastructure, in particular sea defences, transportation, irrigation, drainage, communications, electricity and water supply. The greatest problem of all, however, is restoring the human resource capacity of the country. It is also necessary to strengthen institutions and reinforce environmental initiatives. Strengthening human resource capacity, institutions and the environment is particularly difficult given strong pressures to reduce government expenditure as a central part of the structural adjustment agenda.

This country's government like governments the World over, is charged with the responsibility of providing the overall policy, legislative and institutional framework and conditions within which rising standards of living can be realised. It is all too easy, faced with such poverty and the uphill struggle for development, to forget the fact that the long term success of such an enterprise depends essentially upon the people using wisely the fundamental assets of the country - the natural resource base.

Guyana's wealth lies in the fertility of the soil which produces its principal export crops of rice and sugar and its food crops for domestic consumption. It lies in the wealth beneath the soil, principally in the bauxite, gold and diamonds but also in glass sand, and in a host of minerals and semi-precious stones. The country's riches lie in its extensive forest resources and myriad rivers which carry fish and fertile silt to the populated coastal plain. Guyana's coastal waters produce a rich harvest of fish and crustaceans. Looking at the total ecology of the country the most striking feature is the incredible biodiversity of flora and fauna. As the World grows ever more conscious of the threat to the global environment, the richness of Guyana's environment will become ever more valuable and a source of extensive future eco-tourist potential if well managed. Eco-tourism reflects a growing global interest in the rainforest in particular but natural history in general.

Utilising the natural resource base of the country wisely is the foundation for development. How best to use it wisely is the essential challenge, as this will permit the development to be sustainable and long term. Problems arise because certain ways of utilising some of the natural resources can have an adverse effect on other aspects of natural resource use. If each sector and enterprise pursues its own short term objectives without trying to reconcile these with others' use of the resources then each sector and enterprise runs the risk of having its growth potential threatened by others' actions.

For this reason it is important to prevent an anarchic free-for-all of natural resource exploitation which serves no sector's interests in the long run and moreover does a disservice to the country's overall development efforts. Such a situation may have a profoundly negative effect upon the health and welfare of the population. Herein lies a very important role for government to play, as is widely acknowledged (see for example the World Bank, *World Development Report*) [3]

In this book we examine each sector's operations, its effects upon the environment, and the ways in which it can impact upon the vitality and development potential of other sectors. It is necessary to identify where the potential resource conflicts lie as these can take many forms. Next, if progress is to be made, it is essential for the parties concerned to recognise this situation themselves. They can then be given the opportunity to come together to discuss ways in which these conflicts can begin to be resolved. We try to show how it is possible to adjust current sectoral activities for improved resource utilisation. This should be the subject of open debate, being an important component of the democratic process. An openly conducted process will help create awareness and forge a consensus for a national policy on environment and development. It will also provide the stimulus for putting the necessary legislative and institutional requirements in place. Greater participation and transparency in decision-making will help facilitate a more sustainable pattern of resource use, which should improve the long term developmental return both to the sectors but also overall. We do not dwell in the individual sectoral chapters on the vital social components of the processes. Instead, we have chosen to try to bring these together at the end. However, it is necessary to emphasise that hard evidence on which to base such an analysis is at a premium.

We begin in the interior looking first in individual chapters at mining and then forest resource exploitation. We then move towards the coast looking at agriculture, fishing, human settlement and service provision. A review of industry, transport and energy follows before examining biodiversity, tourism and the Amerindian community. This is followed in a subsequent chapter by a detailed analysis of the challenges to be faced in devising a sustainable development national strategy. This is undertaken in the light of the foregoing analysis and of the Rio Earth Summit and other important international recommendations. One of the most important messages to emerge is the need to tackle as a priority the whole complex of intersectoral issues tied up with coastal zone management. For it is precisely in the coastal zone that the negative impacts of mining and forestry in the interior may be felt and along the coast human settlement, agriculture, industry, transport, coastal protection and fishing compete in their usage of natural resources in limited space. Water is a fundamental resource which quite literally flows between the sectors. The negative effects of one sector's activities are frequently transported to another by the medium of water. Because water is so important it has not been treated as a separate sector but as an integral component of all the sectors.

This need to identify potential resource use conflicts as a first step towards resolving these issues is not a new methodology but it is one which is being pioneered in a number of quarters including by the United Nations Environment Programme. Such an approach has been tried with some success in other parts of Latin America, for example, with regional development river basin planning in Ecuador.[4] In each of the ecosystems of the river basin there was an identification of areas of potential conflict and the actors involved were encouraged to draw their own conclusions based on a preliminary evaluation of the possible negative effects on goods and services of proposed development initiatives. This serves to emphasise the need for intersectoral discussions to be held at the district level as well as nationally. The first step is identifying the conflicts. The second is involving all of the parties concerned in a discussion of the issues in an effort to find a resolution within a national strategy for sustainable development.

Chapter 9 discusses the institutional challenges in the light of the foregoing analysis. All too often institutions reflect the formats and mechanisms of past thinking and are ill-equipped to deal with paradigm shifts. Improving institutional coordination has to be a priority. Finally, Chapter 10 reviews progress in the 1990s, a turbulent decade in Guyana's history but one which finally may help to overcome the shackles of the past. Whilst real economic growth has resulted from the democratisation and policy reform, dangers lie in the seeming attractions of an "anything goes" philosophy to bring in much needed investment and thereby the economic utilisation of the country's rich natural resources. Already a number of environmental and social warnings have been sounded with the Omai mine disaster and the coastal zone flooding in the mid-1990s. There is an enormous social welfare challenge to be faced. The aim has to be to facilitate people's own coping mechanisms. The economy and institutional capacities of the state can at best provide only a minimal welfare safety net function. There will inevitably be winners and losers. The clever strategy is one which tries to facilitate "win-win" situations and thereby maximise electoral and developmental goodwill and support.

Notes

1. T. Ferguson, *Structural Adjustment and Good Governance: The Case of Guyana,* Public Affairs Consultancy Enterprise, Georgetown, 1995.

2. A. Trotz, "Gender, ethnicity and familial ideology in Georgetown, Guyana: Household structure and female labour force participation reconsidered", mimeo, n.d.

3. World Bank, *World Development Report 1992*, WB/UNDP, Washington, 1992.

4. R. Saunier, "Integrated Regional Development Planning, Santiago and Mira River Basins, Ecuador" in C. Conroy and M. Litvinoff (eds), *The Greening of Aid,* Earthscan, London, 1988. pp.162-167.

2 Mining

Mining is second only to agriculture in its importance to the economy of Guyana. It represented around a quarter of GDP in the mid-1990s, but with the rapid expansion of gold mining, particularly at Omai, prospects looked good for future expansion. The central concerns remain how to create a more productive mining sector on the one hand, whilst minimising any potential negative effects upon people and the environment. In this chapter we examine the main mining sub-sectors of bauxite, gold and diamonds and other minerals, the evolution over time of the history of extraction, the economic, social and environmental challenges they have had to face and finally the future opportunities that the mining sector offers.

Bauxite

Bauxite is the most important mining activity. Bauxite deposits run in a wide band parallel to the coast, stretching almost from the Moruka River in the west of the country to the Corentyne River border with Surinam in the east. Guyana's bauxite is whitish rather than pinkish, denoting that it is relatively rich in alumina with relatively low impurities, which makes it suitable for aluminium and the refractory and abrasive industries. Indeed, Guyana is the World's largest producer of calcined bauxite, the highest grade of the mineral.

Commercial exploitation of bauxite began in 1916 when the Aluminium Company of Canada established a subsidiary, the Demerara Bauxite Company, on the Demerara River 70 miles south of Georgetown. Mining operations here grew to such an extent that Linden became the second largest town in the country (pop. 35,000 plus). Another bauxite mining operation began in 1938 at Kwakwani which was run by the Reynolds Company from 1952.

Extensive areas of forest were ripped up in these two locations in almost 80 years of strip mining for bauxite. As the early surface deposits were worked out, the mining went deeper and deeper with up to 70 metres of overburden having to be removed in some locations. The process involves stripping out all of the forest biomass cover, clearing the land with bulldozers before removing the top layer of sand and the layers of sandy clay and clay deeper down. The bauxite ore which is then revealed is removed, to be taken to the processing plants at Linden and Everton where it is crushed and washed. Dried and calcined bauxite is then produced.

Production at the Linden mines grew rapidly, achieving over 100,000 tons a year by the early 1920s and topping the one million ton mark in 1933. The next qualitative leap in the industry came with the building of the alumina plant. From 1961 alumina production began and the important development process of value added had begun within the industry. But the country was never to develop to the final stage of aluminium production, which requires enormous levels of investment and abundant cheap energy.

With the PNC government increasingly espousing socialist policies from the late 1960s, the Alcan owned Linden mines were eventually nationalised in 1971 and Reynolds metals at Kwakwani in 1974. Guymine, the new nationalised company, ran all bauxite mining operations until May 1992, by which time the nationalised company had built up debts of $ 85 million.[1] An Australian company, Minproc Engineering, was then invited by the government to take over the administration of the industry, an interim measure prior to privatisation, as the government needed time to clear the debts. When Guymine was dissolved, two operational arms were formed, Linmine (Linden) and Bermine (Berbice). Eventually, in July 1996, the government announced that the Linden Bauxite Mining Enterprise was up for sale, with production levels in 1995 up to 181,000 tons of ore. From the 1980s onwards, China, the only other producer of non-metallurgical bauxite, had significantly increased its production and exports, reducing Guyana's market share and depressing prices. Nationalisation led to a decline in production given the lack of sufficient local managerial and technological skills, foreign exchange to import spares and replace obsolescent equipment and machinery and the finances for new investment.

Nationalisation had a decidedly negative effect on the country's development, reflected in declining export production. In the 1960s and 1970s Guyana accounted for about four fifths of total World production of calcined bauxite but by the late 1980s this declined to only two fifths.[2] The output of the alumina transformation plant was 320,000 tons in 1975 but rapidly fell to a paltry 29,000 tons by 1983 and all production ceased thereafter.[3] Given a decade of deterioration and technological changes worldwide, the plant is now a write-off. Yet still bauxite remains the country's most significant mineral resource and major foreign exchange earner. In 1990 it accounted for 37% of total merchandise exports and 12% of registered GDP. At its peak there were 7 mines operating at the Linden site but by the early 1990s it was down to only 3.[4] The enterprise as a whole was operating at half its capacity.

As a result of the lack of new investment over the two decades of state control, there were serious development setbacks and considerable environmental costs. An astonishing 250,000 tons of bauxite was being lost each year in the production process as a result of out-dated and inefficient technology. This poured out of the processing factory chimney daily as dust, coating the surrounding countryside, houses, gardens and people. The technology is readily available not only to reduce the local pollution and improve the health of the workers and surrounding population but also to prevent this loss of production and profit. Introducing the technology to save the current loss of a quarter of a million tons of processed bauxite a year could possibly recoup the cost of the new technology and prove far more cost effective than digging an additional equivalent amount out of the ground. The existing plant developed in a very "ad hoc" manner which contributed to inefficiency. In particular failure to renew old equipment also meant continuing energy inefficiency with attendant high foreign exchange costs.

Originally the plant was equipped with scrubbers, but following nationalisation "In time, what people did not fully understand, they by-passed", in the words of a senior manager.[5] A special crew operated the scrubbers for a while but soon they ceased to function. The drying of the bauxite creates considerable dust. An electrostatic precipitator fitted onto the drier would both extract and reclaim the dust which is of a high quality and a machine can profitably reconstitute this. But this requires a heavy initial capital investment which the government was unable to provide. The processing plant was also inundated with scrap metal representing a health and safety hazard and a lost development opportunity for scrap metal recycling, something which used to occur regularly in the past.

In spite of the enormous health and safety risks associated with the industry, the noise, dust, heat, danger from mining and processing machinery, no study was ever carried out in recent times either on the health effects on the workforce or on the surrounding population.[6] Over long periods of exposure airborne bauxite dust causes lung irritation and promotes bronchial infections. No information is available either on the possible extent of aluminium contamination of water supplies.

Mine rehabilitation has been virtually ignored over the past decades. In theory the removal of overburden from a new site is used to fill in the old excavations. But given all of the problems in the industry over recent years, all efforts were directed to production not reclamation. Hence the overburden was simply dumped in waste mountains. The resulting landscape looks like a science fiction film set, with towering sand mountains and pools of ground water and precipitation. Biomass recolonisation is extremely slow on these sandy rolling plains. The combination of strip mining and poor soil quality leaves a woeful legacy for future constructive land utilisation. The only efforts made to date to utilise the mined out land was a fisheries experiment in the excavation pools, said to be unsuccessful because of the acidic nature of the waters.

Employment creation and wealth generation was a clear plus factor for the people in the area. Linden acted as a growth pole to attract people away from the coast. Initially people commuted back to Georgetown but eventually there was a sufficient community and cultural centre of gravity that people stayed, at first over the weekend and later for good. The new generation has its roots in Linden rather than on the coast and this marks a significant step forward in local community self-awareness. A sense of permanence and community is important if local pressure is to build up to demand a clean up the environment, in particular where the lives and well-being of children are concerned.

As economic pressures on the bauxite industry grew, retrenchment took place with the workforce being halved dramatically from 6,000 to 3,000 by the early 1990s, inevitably causing community upheavals. Traditionally, the company and the town had a symbiotic relationship. The town expanded to house the growing workforce and to meet its needs and the company assumed a certain responsibility for service provision and community facilities. Traditionally the company provided the water and electricity to the town, assisted the government with roads and looked after health and education. In recent years the relationship has come under increasing strain. As the fortunes of the bauxite industry declined skilled and talented people were attracted away. Pressures on the urban environment are beginning to grow, as the timber industry expands and the road through the area to Brazil is slowly being completed. Linden is a major pole of settlement but housing provision is severely inadequate. Whilst the family household size is around 5 in Georgetown it is 7 in Linden. The serious housing shortage encourages squatting with all of the attendant problems of inadequate facilities and poor sanitation. Serious urban environmental problems are apparent, particularly in the poorer suburbs of Wismar and Christianburg. Squatter settlements are vulnerable both to land slips and to houses collapsing under the force of high winds.

The bauxite industry seems set to grow in the 1990s with C.A. Dayeo de Construciones of Venezuela being involved in a venture to mine 1.4 million tons of bauxite annually to be sold to Interalumina of Venezuela and a subsidiary of Reynold Metals.

The crucial environment and development issues facing the bauxite industry are:

• New investment, to improve output, energy efficiency, reduce the escape of bauxite dust into the atmosphere and implement land reclamation;

- Clearing up the scrap on site and using it for recycling;
- Improving health and safety of the workforce and of the surrounding community.

The bauxite industry has contributed positively to surrounding human settlements by providing employment and services but negatively concerning pollution.

The negative effects on other sectors include:

- Loss of forestry resources;
- Loss of land for other land uses;
- Damage to the watershed of the sandy rolling plain which supplies the conservancies with the water so necessary for agricultural production;
- Possible river pollution.

New investors in the industry will need to be encouraged to follow good environmental practices in particular concerning land reclamation, health and safety in the workplace and minimising pollution of the air, water and soils.

Gold and diamonds

In Guyana most of the deposits lie to the west of the Essequibo River along its tributaries and further into the hinterland. The gold and diamonds are located in gravels on the bedrock covered by sand and in the flats of rivers, past and present. There are also terrace and hill deposits near the river beds and flats. The mining is carried out by excavating the river banks and dredging the river beds and banks.   Official statistics of gold and diamond production have massively underestimated the scale of operations as low official fixed prices resulted in extensive smuggling. When the Gold Board agreed to pay market rates of exchange for gold in 1990, official production figures doubled to 39,000 oz over the previous year.[7] In 1991 production continued rising to 59,154 oz, earning US$ 18 million, and in 1992 was almost 80,000 oz.[8] The liberalisation of investment policy is attracting new foreign investors into the industry. By far the biggest venture is at Omai involving the Canadian group Cambio (owning 60%) and Gold Star Resources (owning 35%) in a US$ 150 million plus investment. The government will own 5%. The mine began operating in 1993 and is said to be the largest single metal mine in Latin America and the Caribbean. Production at Omai during the peak first three year period was estimated to be 250,000 oz which would double existing annual production.[9]

The search for boundless riches through the discovery of gold and diamonds has been the quest of miners throughout the ages. The reality for the "porkknockers" (the local name for the small scale miners) of Guyana is far more prosaical. Thousands work the river banks deep in the interior of the country with nothing more than a pick and shovel, the sweat of their brow, a pan, a sluice, plastic hose and a can to boil off the mercury from the gold amalgam. Many families find employment here. Although the number of miners are not known with any accuracy Walrond's figure of 5,000 should be seen as a lower estimate.[10] The people know the countryside and some could become excellent eco-tourist guides in the future.

Mining takes different forms. The small scale operations are run by a few itinerant miners who dig pits at the side of the rivers passing the excavated material through a sluice box. The waste is discharged into the river or onto the surrounding river banks. A slightly more sophisticated system uses a high pressure water jet to slurry the overburden and gold bearing gravels. Following the gravity separation process mercury is mixed in with the concentrate and it amalgamates with the gold. The mixture is squeezed through a cloth, the mercury thus separated is rebottled for future use. The remaining gold-mercury amalgam is finally separated by heating.

There is certainly a cost to the environment from these activities, notably in a degree of mercury pollution which can find its way into the food chain, as has happened in Brazil, in river siltation, and of course the health risk to miners working in precarious conditions. Recent research suggests that in Brazil environmental degradation from industrial mining tends not to be as great as from "garimpo" (small scale) operations.[11] The reason for this is, in part, that government controls over the large companies through demands for Environment Impact Assessments (EIAs) and reclamation plans are more feasible than over the myriad "garimpeiros". In Brazil, over a million or more people are engaged in small scale mining, so the collective effect is considerable.[12] But in Guyana the simple technology employed and small scale nature of the operations thus far, limits to some degree the negative environmental effects and guarantees a labour intensive, employment creating effort. There are signs of a growing influx of Brazilian small scale miners entering the country and this could soon alter the situation. They are already operating in the Pakaraima Mountains, the Wenama River in the Kanukus, Marudi Mountains south of the Rupununi and along the border at the head of the Essequibo. If the economy picks up in Guyana as the liberalisation measures continue and with the completion of the road to Brazil, it is possible that a further influx of Brazilian miners might occur which could increase the mercury water pollution problem. However, the Brazilians have developed a cheap new retort that can cut mercury emissions by 50%, catching far more mercury for reuse. It would clearly be of great value to ensure the spread of this technology in Guyana as it will both increase profitability for the miners and reduce pollution.

Potential problems involved with an influx of Brazilian miners include cultural conflicts, a rise in prostitution and alcoholism within Amerindian communities, smuggling and an even weaker degree of control by central government. The Guyanese Defence Force has evicted some immigrant miners from these areas.

Research by Indal Rambajan reveals a further environmental health problem associated with small scale itinerant mining.[13] After twenty years absence, falciparum malaria came back with a vengeance in the mid-1980s to North West Guyana, accompanied by a significant rise in vivax cases. In essence the probability is that the itinerant miners brought this chloroquine-resistant strain from the Rupununi River in southern Guyana up to the Cuyuni/Mozaruni/Potaro area in 1985 and it moved onwards to the North West region.

Undoubtedly damaging to the environment are the missile suction-pump dredging operations along the natural water courses and constructed paddocks, normally by venturi and gravel pump suction. The suction dredge was originally introduced in 1958, using a diver to control the suction hose. The technology was rapidly adopted. From the mid 1980s a winch was introduced to operate the suction system hence the dredgers no longer relied on a diver working in potentially hazardous conditions.[14] The dredgers suck material into the floating washing plant, discharging the tailings overboard. Watkin and Woolford have pointed out that the dredgers are unable to control where the discharge goes, hence this impedes the river flow and navigation channels as tailings are deposited all over the place.[15]

It is significant for the developmental value added, that the construction of the missile dredgers is taking place within Guyana. They are designed for mobility in difficult areas of access, for safety by eliminating diver operations and for their suitability in mining old river channels. A Brazilian designer dredge, which has worse environmental effects and was eventually banned in that country is now being used in Guyana.

A number of problems have emerged with this method of mining and we will examine the most important of these known thus far. It is important to qualify this account with the phrase 'known thus far" as in fact very little is known thus far because of inadequate monitoring and control facilities. The remote Upper Mazaruni Mining District in the north west of Guyana near the Venezuela border is a centre of this mining activity, particularly along the river banks. In the late 1980s the introduction of missile suction-pump dredges here led to widespread concern among the local community about dangers to the environment, local economy, and social fabric.[16] In the interior of Guyana the rivers are the lifelines of the people, providing drinking water, the transport highways and through fishing provide a major source of protein intake. Following the introduction of missile dredging, villagers forty miles downstream from the mining operations at Jawalla complained that they could no longer drink water from the river or wash their clothes in the water. River transportation was also impeded, particularly in the low water season. Riverside forest clearance and missile dredging operations from the mining result in mud, forest debris and pilings congregating in the river. River travel is becoming increasingly hazardous, particularly at night, a practice which is normal in this area. As the river channels are widened the river grows shallower slowing the flow. At low water deposits of sand and stone tailings virtually block parts of the river. Silt deposits have risen significantly during periods of flooding. Local people report an increase of accidents and of mosquitoes breeding as a result of the stagnant pools of water. A further effect of the missile dredgers, as yet unquantified, is on the small scale mining operations, which use the traditional divers whose work may be impaired or become more hazardous.

Missile dredging operations also affect local fishing, as mining depositions cover traditional rocky spawning grounds. Downstream of the mining operations in the Middle Mazaruni the fishermen who supply freshwater fish, in particular "paku" and "lukanoni" to the coastal population may have their livelihoods affected.

The negative visual effects of the mining operations have an impact upon the eco-tourist potential, the local community's appreciation of its environment and on the cultural values of the local population. Access to the treasures of the Upper Mazaruni, the rock paintings and Chichi falls may be terminally impaired by the transformation of the river, in the words of some local residents, into a "mud-choked gutter".[17]

The economic impact of the missile dredge mining upon the local economy and society has been even more wideranging. Serious distortions have emerged in the local economy as labourers were recruited to clear riverbanks at a wage of G.D. 1,000 per day when the existing average daily wage in the area was GD 65. This fuelled a massive price inflation in local stores to the detriment of those not involved in mining, causing major socio-economic disruptions within the local Amerindian communities.

As a result of letters of complaint sent to government by the local Christian community there was a visit by the Environment Unit of the Guyana Agency for Health Sciences, Education, Environment and Food Policy (GAHEF). A GAHEF report on the field visit in 1990 stated that: "Beyond Jawalla, a scene which is not believing to the eye can be viewed."[18] The river was virtually blocked with tailings, mostly of stone not easily washed

18

downstream. Huge 30 metre deep craters had been dug into the river bank. It is fortunate from the viewpoint of river transportation that most of the Amerindian settlements are downstream from the mining operations, as it is mainly the miners who have to try to navigate upstream. The miners themselves confess that they have no solution to these problems at present.

Another area seriously affected is the Potaro River and the Tumatumari Mines, which have suffered from a long history of gold mining operations with a cumulative long term effect contributing to the current problems. The missile dredging here involves excavating the river bank 2 metres by 2 metres following hand clearing of the vegetation. Frequently half a dozen dredgers or more have been working in proximity, and here the negative effects are particularly pronounced.[19] In some cases the sacred burial grounds of the Amerindian communities have been disturbed.

All of the S.D. issues of the multi-sectoral usage of river resource come together starkly on the Potaro river. Higher upstream is the famous Kaieteur National Park whose central attraction is the 741 feet drop Falls. Discussions with the Japanese have taken place about a possible hydropower development just below the falls on the Kuribrong and Potaro rivers, concerning the Amalia-Kaieteur Hydropower Development scheme.

GAHEF and the Guyana Geology and Mines Commission (GGMC), the two government institutions most involved at the beginning of the 1990s, were immensely limited in their environmental investigative capacity. First, there was the enormous cost financially and in scarce staff time of launching an expedition to the interior for monitoring operations. Second, there was no capacity within Guyana to have any of the river water samples analysed at the Institute of Applied Science and Technology (IAST), given inadequate equipment.

Within these limitations, in the middle of 1991 GAHEF was able to summarize its findings on the environmental effects of the mining. The physical effects of the gold mining included land disturbances, changes in water courses and in water quality. The health effects included an upsurge in malaria from the 1980s and the as yet unquantified effects on miners and local residents of extensive mercury use.

Gold mining has serious environmental effects destroying river bank vegetation and the banks themselves, which can change the river channel morphology affecting the habitat of fish and fishing productivity, navigation of the rivers, supply of potable water and erosion of river banks. Additional problems include a negative visual impact on the environment and economic and social disruptions to local Amerindian communities.

A growing concern led to studies being commissioned by the Guyana Geology and Mines Commission (GGMC) through the Commonwealth Secretariat. The first report came up with a series of recommendations that it

19

suggested should be implemented in three phases.[20] In a first phase, river claim miners should be asked to leave a 50 foot wide navigable channel at low water mark where natural conditions permitted. After mining, tailings should be distributed to a maximum height outside of the channel to about 2 feet above the low water mark and simple gauge boards should be installed in mining areas. For land claim mining, all trees should be felled away from the river and removed from the river. If possible a commercial use should be found for these trees. In a second phase, for land claim mining tailings should be deposited against the newly created river bank sloping towards the river. In phase 3 after about 12 months all river bank mining should be prohibited until a mineral resource survey ascertains if the resource exists. Then a mining plan would have to be submitted and approved by GGMC.

A second study commissioned by the Commonwealth Secretariat covered some of the same ground and recommended that environmental control strategies be developed for various small pit and river based mining operations.[21] There should be exploration and delineation of gold bearing deposits along rivers and adjacent lands to eliminate unnecessary riverine mining and river zones for exclusion of dredge mining should be established. Legal provision was required to prohibit mining within 30 metres inland from the generally accepted low water mark for specific regions of the river. Efforts should be made to ensure efficient mining and processing procedures to reduce environmental impact. All claims using missile dredges should file annual operating and management plans. A special recommendation was made for the Upper Mazaruni River area which the report acknowledged to be particularly bad, saying that this was the area most resembling the intensive gold mining of the "garimpeiros" in Brazil. It suggests that future ownership and exploration of gold claims in this area be restricted to "bona fide" residents of more than three years standing. Yet, as already is happening, this does not prevent Brazilians from renting claims in the North-West from local owners. Further necessary measures include strengthening the human and material resource capacity for monitoring mining operations and analysing samples.

Watkin and Woolford spell out some on the practical difficulties on improving environmental practices in alluvial gold mining in Guyana.[22] The first concerns the geological data. In many areas the distribution of gold bearing gravels is not known or may not be in the public domain hence much of the mining is speculative and pointlessly destructive. The most serious potential polluting effect comes from mercury and whilst to date its effects are likely to be limited (but we have no hard data), as the industry expands close monitoring will be needed, in particular concerning sedimentation effects and land disturbances. Watkin and Woolford explain the overall problem thus:

The difficulty with finding solutions is, that by its very definition, the small mine cannot support sophisticated environmental impact assessment, exploration programmes, or sophisticated equipment or procedures for processing. This means that either governmental organisations will have to aid the small miners or small miners will have to form cooperative groupings to benefit from economies of scale as they seek to address environmental problems.[23]

In order to provide help for the small miner to implement environmental management and control procedures, Watkin and Woolford suggest that the Hoyte Government already accepted that it might provide:

1) Technical assistance through the establishment of research and the provision of technical advisory services in order to:
   (a) Make the local miner aware of the cost-effective technology he can acquire to ensure compliance with environmental regulations;
   (b) Design systems to ameliorate environmental damage to land and water resulting from mining operations;
   (c) Ensure that environmental regulations are based on sound scientific data and to analyse the economic impact of the regulations on the mining industry.
2) Education and training of miners in order to:
   (a) Make the miner aware of the environmental requirements governing the operations;
   (b) Make the miner aware that technology is available to ensure compliance with the regulations;
   (c) Make the miner aware that his operations depend on public consent.
3) A public awareness programme in order to:
   (a) Keep the public informed of the effects being undertaken to ensure compliance by the miners and of the successes in achieving the goal of minimising environmental damage.

Environmental management and control systems for the small-scale gold mining industry thus far show no signs of being implemented. A multi-disciplinary technical advisory team was meant to be drawing up a short EIA compliance document including "a standardised operating plan outlining the modus operandi including on-going exploration, deforestation, topsoil conservation and overburden removal, impoundment of tailings and rehabilitation of the mined-out areas."[24] It was meant to recommend areas to be closed to prospecting and mining, with tests to be carried out on a number of rivers and help given for the optimum design of mining systems, a modified dredge design was to be tested and an environmental bond was proposed for the operation of a dredge to ensure compliance.

The central problem in all of this is obviously the necessary commitment to ensure that action will be taken. Here as in other sectors, direct economic interests of those in power and of their important supporters can seriously dilute any commitment to clean up the environment if this puts profits at stake. All governments, in Guyana and elsewhere, are faced with this dilemma. Ownership of a missile dredge represents a manageable level of capital investment for a Guyanese investor. In addition, the institutional, human resource and financial capacity to ensure compliance has to be in place. Such problems exist not only for mining but for *all* sectors.

The new large scale gold mining activities raise other environmental concerns. The massive new venture at Omai is a huge open-pit gold mine, involving clear felling with state of the art processing. Cyanide is used to recover gold, using conventional vat leaching techniques in a carbon-in-pulp circuit. As large foreign multinationals are involved here, it is to be hoped that consideration of their own environmental image combined with a clear legislative framework by the government and with the checking mechanism of an informed and alert media, environment NGOs and the general public will ensure that the best international standards will be maintained and any lapses are revealed. Under the Mining Act, before a mining license is granted, a feasibility study had to be submitted which included an EIA with the GGMC forwarding this to GAHEF for its approval, later the Environment Protection Agency assumed this role.

The first big test came quite quickly. Omai's production levels were indeed spectacular. The figures for gold production nationally rose dramatically from 79,579 ozs in 1992, to 309,772 ozs in 1993 and 375,456 ozs in 1994.[25] This national economic success story was rudely interrupted in August of the following year, 1995, when levels of the waste water reservoir dam were raised higher than the limits set by engineers. The holding dam collapsed and released an estimated three million cubic meters of slurry containing cyanide and heavy metals into the Omai river.[26] There was considerable media interest and public debate, with the government closing down the mining operations for a period of time. There were no recorded human fatalities at the time but a significant upset to the local fishing industry and widespread concern over drinking water amongst the communities affected, particularly in Bartica. Significantly the lack of baseline data made the task of measuring potential increases in pollution levels extremely difficult. Public debate focused on the extent to which there were adequate environmental monitoring regulations and more generally on the working conditions. The government referred to the event as an "environmental disaster".

All the diamonds mined are alluvial in river channels. Suction dredging is used to retrieve diamonds as well as gold. Given the small scale and dispersed nature of the diamond operations little negative environmental impact is experienced.

Other minerals

Minerals currently being mined include silica sand, shells, kaolin and other clays, semi-precious stones and stone aggregate. In the future this list could extend to potash, feldspar and manganese and many other minerals have been located.[27] Key environmental issues include deforestation for silica sand mining and stone quarries, whilst shell mining can undermine coastal protection and negatively impact on local flora and fauna. The shell beach environment problems seem set to increase. Hence there is significant disruption of the nesting sites of four species of turtle at Shell Beach by Waini Point. As the imperative for agriculture expansion increases, the demand for lime from shell mining will increase to help neutralise the predominantly acid soils in the agricultural land. Sand extraction from beaches and estuaries for the construction industry is one more causal factor in the progressive destruction of the mangrove belt.

Future opportunities

The current privatisation initiatives of state mining companies in Latin America generally provide opportunities for the diffusion of both profitable and environmentally-sound best practice in metals production.[28] Guyana could also benefit from such initiatives if the right precautions are taken. Tougher international laws and standards both internationally and nationally do not necessarily create problems for new mining initiatives. One recent study concluded:

> It seems unlikely that environmental policies are a major factor in determining where a mining company will target exploration and subsequent investment activities. Moreover, secure geological potential and political stability (which might imply clear and constant environmental policies) are also considered important factors ... [29]

Problems arise with the old and inefficient operations. Obliging these to take on additional costs for improved pollution control will frequently push them over the edge from profit to loss, with the unhappy prospect of increasing unemployment. As Warhurst explains:

> The policy challenge is therefore, how to keep firms sufficiently dynamic to be able to afford to clean-up their pollution and generate economic wealth through innovation. The achievement of improved production efficiency and environmental management will, in turn, be dependent upon the extent to which technology transfer and training clauses are built into new joint ventures, investment arrangements or loan conditions, whatever the financial arrangements.[30]

An interesting Caribbean example relevant to Guyana concerns Alcan's bauxite production operations in Jamaica. In an effort to reduce the environmental impact of its operations it supported the local university to find a solution to the disposal of its red mud sludge. They developed a system of sun-drying and stacking the material in bricks in less obtrusive piles. Whilst this will reduce future water pollution, it may still increase air pollution through the dust it creates.[31] The important point, however, is that initiatives can be taken using local human and institutional resources.

Figure 2.1 provides a general overview of the effects of the mining process on the environment.

The Omai disaster marked a turning point in people's awareness of the potential dangers associated with the rapid expansion of mining activities. Warnings were given earlier by GEMCO when smaller spillages occurred.[32] As a result of the major spillage of August 1995 the government not only closed down the mining operations until early the following year but it also set up a Commission of Enquiry. Marcus Colchester captures the dilemmas well:

> ... while efforts to push through new environmental legislation and set up more adequate government institutions to regulate the runaway mining industry have gained some impetus from the disaster, pressure from foreign mining companies has also intensified.[33]

Indeed by late 1996, mining grants and licenses had been granted covering a tenth of the country with other exploratory areas being granted, indeed in 1996 the number of large scale mining licences being granted was running at more than double the rate of the previous year.[34]

Notes

1. *Financial Times,* 15 May 1992.

2. See World Bank, *Guyana: A Framework for Economic Recovery*, World Bank, Washington DC., 1985, p.18 and *Financial Times*, 15 May 1992.

3. World Bank (1985), *op. cit*, pp.144-145.

4. Interview with Jimmy Hamilton, long time employee at the mine and the local repository of its oral history, Linden, Guyana, 15 January 1992.

5. Interview with Walter Melvine, Head of Financial Administration, Guymine, Linden, 15 January 1992.

6. Interview with Keith Hall, Senior Hospital Administrator, Linden, 15 January 1992.

7. Economist Intelligence Unit, *Guyana Country Profile 1991-92*, EIU 1991/2, p.17.

8. EIU, *Guyana: Country Profile 1993/94*, EIU, 1993, p.17.

9. World Bank, *Guyana: Recent Economic Developments, Medium Term Prospects and Background to the Government's Project List 1992-5*, World Bank, 24 June 1991, p.17.

10. G.W. Walrond, "Exploration in Guyana". Paper No 38 in *Proceedings of first International Symposium on Mineral Exploration Programmes*, Madrid, 1989.

11. M. Hanai, "Gold mining in Brazil - environmental and social impacts" in *Mining and Environment Research Network Newsletter* No 2, April 1992, p.8.

12. J.A. Machado, "Los hurones de la selva" in *Amazonia, la selva cercade*, El Pais, Madrid, 1990. Note that some accounts put the total far less at between 300 to 500,000. See S. Hecht and A. Cockburn, *The Fate of the Forest*, Penguin, London, 1990, p.143.

13. I. Rambajan, "Highly prevalent falciparum malaria in North West Guyana: its development history and control problems", *Bulletin of PAHO*, Vol 28, No 3, 1994.

14. E.M. Watkin and W.H. Woolford, *Alluvial Gold Mining in Guyana: Environmental Aspects.* A paper presented at the Institution of Mining and Metallurgy, Minerals, Metals and the Environment Conference, Manchester 1992.

15. *ibid.*

16. See *An Association of village groups for Christian action in the Mazaruni river, Guyana,* letter to the Commissioner, Guyana Geology and Mines Commission', Georgetown, 20 August 1989.

17. *ibid.*

18. GAHEF Environment Unit *Report on visit to Upper Mazaruni District, 23-27 March 1990.* GAHEF, Georgetown, 1990.

19. GAHEF Environment Unit, *Report on a site visit to Potaro River (Tumatumari Mines), 21 October 1989.*

20. Dept. of Mines, Western Australia *Report on the Technological and Operational Aspects of Dredge and Small Scale Open Pit Gold and Diamond Mining in the Co-operative Republic of Guyana,* a report commissioned by the Commonwealth Secretariat, December 1990.

21. Creme and Warner, *A Review of Environmental Aspects of Dredge and Small Pit Mining Operations,* made in consultation with Commonwealth Secretariat for Government of Co-operative Republic of Guyana, January 1991.

22. Watkins and Woolford (1992) *op. cit.*

23. *ibid.*

24. *ibid.*

25. Economist Intelligence Unit, Guyana. *Country Profile 1995-96,* EIU, 1996, p.20.

26. *The Ecologist*, Vol 25, No 5, 1995.

27. See Guyana Geology and Mines Commission, *Mineral Exploration Map of Guyana*, Scale 1:1,000,000, 1987.

28. A. Warhurst, *"Towards Environmental Best-Practice in Metals Production,"* paper prepared for Second Mining and Environment Research Network Workshop, Wiston House, Steyning, UK, September 1992, p.2

29. A. Warhurst, *Environmental Management in Mining and Mineral Processing in Developing Countries: Enterprise Behaviour and National Policies*, Science Policy Research Unit, Sussex, 1991, pp.22.

30. A. Warhurst (1992), *op.cit*, p.2.

31. *ibid*, p.19.

32. P. Williams, *"Institutional framework for land management in Guyana,"* a paper given at the conference on Environment and Development in Guyana, Centre for Developing Areas Research, Royal Holloway, University of London, 7 May 1997.

33. M. Colchester, "Guyana: fragile frontier", *Race and Class*, Vol 38, No 4, 1997, p.46.

34. *ibid*, p.47.

3 Forestry

Overview

Guyana is one of the few countries in the world whose tropical forest is virtually intact. Nine tenths of the Commonwealth Caribbean's total commercial forest resources are found in Guyana. Estimates suggest Guyana has approximately 3.6 million ha of exploitable forest and a further 10.4 million ha of exploitable but currently not accessible forest.[1] Figures for the total forested area of the country vary widely from 16 million ha[2] to 19 million ha.[3] The area allocated for commercial exploitation had 10 large and 250 medium and small operators in 1991[4], yet it remained little developed at the beginning of the decade in spite of enormous potential. It employed at that time about 10,000 people, produced 94,000m3 of timber according to official statistics, provided US$ 4 million in exports which comprised 2.5% of GDP.[5] As royalties had to be paid on the logged timber the figures are undoubtedly an underestimate. Government capacity to monitor company operations is very weak given limited resources, as in all government sectors.

Historically there had been no clear felling of timber within the industry, rather felling of selected species, such as greenheart and purpleheart, was undertaken. Clear felling did occur but to facilitate other forms of land use such as agriculture, mining and settlement.

Sawmills worked well below capacity with obsolete equipment. Timber extraction was constrained by low dynamism in the sector, which reflected the overall stagnation in the economy during the socialist experiment of the post-independence era. In addition there was both limited availability of commercially exploitable species and limited access to these. Half a dozen species accounted for two thirds of timber production with 20 additional species accounting for the rest. Yet there are over 1,000 tree species in the country. Greenheart is by far the most important commercial species, and is used extensively in building. It is endemic to Guyana and is excellent for housing and marine construction. Until the 1990s commercial exploitation of timber was predominantly a small scale Guyanese affair. But with the structural adjustment programme and divestiture of state holdings all this was to change dramatically. Large foreign companies moved into the industry. The selling of the forests began in earnest.

New foreign logging initiatives

The first and most internationally publicised case concerned government divestiture of Demerara Woods Limited. A deal was agreed with the Beaverbrook group to purchase the company for £9.7 million in February 1991. The new company was renamed Demerara Timbers Ltd (DTL).[6] The Beaverbrook group put its own small specialist team in to re-evaluate the timber resource base and sold it on in June 1991 to the United Dutch Group (UDG) for £62.5 million, pocketing on paper over £50 million in profit, by having it massively revalued following the carrying out of a more detailed inventory.[7] By July 1991, when the first part of the purchase price of £9.7 million was actually to be paid to the Government of Guyana the United Dutch Group placed an estimated value on DTL of £74 million.

This case highlights the serious problem existing in government's lack of capacity to effectively evaluate the natural resource base to be leased and to negotiate agreements to provide an adequate return. A key consideration throughout has to be establishing the ground rules for sustainable harvesting of the tropical timber resource.

The company has a 50 year lease on timber concessions on 440,000 hectares of forest. By the following year DTL had rapidly moved up to become the major timber exporter in the country, it was previously seventh.[8] All was far from well however, as the DTL parent company, the UDG was suspended from the Amsterdam Stock Exchange on 2 March 1993.[9] The UDG was a holding company that administered interests in a wide variety of companies, including Wembley football stadium in England, it carried an enormous debt and its share price had dropped spectacularly from 9 Dutch guilders to 0.30 guilders a share.[10] As Lord Beaverbrook was paid for his earlier transaction largely in shares in UDG, he also suffered the fallout and also went bankrupt. Critics of the deal could be forgiven for thinking that the spirits of the forest had struck back.

Whilst the Government of Guyana may have lost out financially on this particular divestiture, the group that eventually bought this concession expressed a commitment to sustainable harvesting. Being a Dutch/Danish owned company it was at least open to investigation and pressure for environmental good practice from its home constituency. The University of Utrecht in The Netherlands in collaboration with the University of Guyana established the Tropenbos project at Mabura Hill in the middle of the DTL concession. One of the aims of the project is to establish effective ground rules for sustainable harvesting.[11]

DTL to their credit asked Tropenbos for sustainable harvesting guidelines. The results of the studies being carried out at Mabura Hill will take some time to be completed. In the interim Tropenbos recommended that the system developed by the University of Wageningen in Surinam, known as CELOS be adopted. This recommends cutting no more than 20 cu metres per ha every 20 to 25 years.[12] This is said to represent no more than 7% to 8% of the total cubic meterage. Such a regime, it is said, should not have long term negative effects as long as good practices are adhered to, such as ensuring maintenance of closed canopy cover, not cutting near watercourses etc.

A second massive 50 year logging concession has been granted to a Korean and Malaysian venture, whose Guyana operation goes under the company name of Barama. The Korean company is Sunkyong and the Malaysian company is Samling Timbers. The main concession of 4.127 million acres, is in the north west near the Venezuela border.

The concession covers the production and export of logs, sawn lumber, veneer, plywood and other wood and wood related products.[13] Clause 2 of the agreement states that the concession area will operate under sustainable yield management over a 25 year cutting cycle. Nothing is specified as to the system to be employed, only that a forestry management plan would be submitted covering the first three years of the concession within one year of the signing of the agreement. The company employed the Edinburgh Centre for Tropical Forests (ECTF) to help carry out its management plan. The planning exercise would be repeated over subsequent three year periods. If the annual extraction target is not achieved the balance can be carried over. Given the need to maintain forest canopy cover to preserve the forest system this agreement leaves a great deal open. First there is the criteria to be adopted for sustainable yield management and second, the carry over factor can threaten the viability of the forest system.

As investment inducements, the company was granted a comprehensive 5 year tax holiday automatically renewable for a further 5 years. Any future changes in the tax laws it is stipulated, can only work to the company's benefit. The only direct financial benefit to the country is the royalty. The influential local newspaper *The Catholic Standard* suggested that the deal was greatly in Barama's favour.[14] Most surprising was the fact that the rate was fixed for twenty years with no provision for the rate to rise with inflation. Other loggers (mainly Guyanese) will lose their rights to operate in the concession area. The President of the Forest Products Association, Mr John Williams, complained that the Barama Company had a 10% to 15% advantage over local timber producers.[15] The clause in the contract protecting the rights of indigenous people remained vague. In particular the company would be exempt from any future laws which might improve the existing rights of Amerindian communities.

Once the terms of the agreement had been published in the local press it provoked considerable debate. The sheer size of the concession, about 6,000 square miles, representing almost 8% of the country, was huge by any standards. Foreign companies such as Barama and DTL were being given concessions not available to local companies. Yet the Vice-Chairman of the Sunkyong group on his visit to Guyana suggested that within five years Barama could be earning Guyana $100 million per annum. It would in addition involve local employment and training, a hospital would be built and medical care provided free of charge.

The newly formed Guyana Environmental Monitoring and Conservation Organisation (GEMCO) took the initiative to reveal the terms of the contract to the media. In an open letter to President Cheddi Jagan in February 1993 it complained that logging operations were proceeding before the ECTF had carried out its impact studies. Dr Kenneth King, who advised President Hoyte when the Barama deal was signed produced a defence of the agreement in the press exchanges.[16] The North West district of the concession had not been exploited by local timber producers he argued, because it was a different and remote form of forest. It was more suitable to plywood and veneer production than harvesting of greenheart. Access and building infrastructure on the wet spongy soils of the area is expensive and the investment necessary to build a plywood mill is high. Hence local Guyanese investment had not been an option for exploiting this area of Guyana's forests, according to Dr King. Guyana's political history has been such, King argued, that Jagan and Burnham's socialist leanings did not make the country an attractive investment opportunity. Under Hoyte, efforts had been made to attract international investment and the conditions negotiated for Barama were similar to those in other developing countries.

GEMCO followed up on its initial critique of the agreement with an open letter to the President's Adviser on Science, Technology and Environment.[17] Criticisms involved the generosity of the concessions, loss of national sovereignty, long term negative cultural and economic impacts of unrestrained exploitation of the country's natural resources, the lack of attention to wildlife and environment protection, and the absence of credible mechanisms for monitoring company operations. GEMCO suggests that contracts agreed with DTL and Omai Gold Mines could have equally objectionable provisions. It ends by offering that "GEMCO is prepared to assist government in whatever way it can to promote informed, independent assessment of current ventures."[18] Furthermore, it states that all future investment proposals should be subjected to public scrutiny.

There is clearly a role that could usefully be played by an environment NGO in the evaluation of contract provisions and also in monitoring company compliance. The NGO can function as a consultancy, using the professional expertise of its members, usually drawn from the academic and civil service professions to provide independent advice. Such a consultancy helps provide a valuable additional source of income to help maintain existing professional expertise within low paid government service and academia. It also demonstrates that there is a viable career track for environmental expertise. The debate over the royalty rate of the logged timber is linked to similar concerns for the employees of the relevant state structures. A Royalty Review Committee established in 1991 recommended significant royalty increases in order to support the government Forestry Commission, whose budget for 1991 was G$ 51 million whilst the royalty revenue was only G$ 31 million.[19]

By the late 1990s some further evidence was coming to light about certain areas of forest exploitation. The Edinburgh Centre for Tropical Forests had been commissioned by Barama to do research on what is a sustainable rate of logging and LTS International Ltd. Edinburgh has been doing the actual monitoring. By the late 1990s research results suggested that the road building was having the greatest effect; roads are made of clay not laterite and given the heavy rain (3,000 mm per year) need a high crown and 25 to 30 meters clearing on either side of the road along with drainage putting in, which clearly will interfere with fauna migration.[20] Roads take up an astonishing 6% of the huge concession area which involves clear felling.

According to LTS International Edinburgh, apart from the road construction the key damage is caused not by the felling nor using the skidders to get the timber out, but rather the impact of the bulldozers and tractors, whereas other methods such as the use of winches may do less harm.[21] Barama are felling four trees per hectare but damaging 19 or 20 other tress, about 25% of the remaining stand. In practice the size of the timber is smaller than expected, hence the company appears to be operating at only about 60% of the norm they had established. Supporters of the scheme say that this is an area of poor forest, without the traditionally high value species, but it is suitable for plywood production. However, trees have to be of a certain diameter even to be useful for plywood production. LTS International suggest that the current rate of logging is not too bad in terms of sustainability but that we will only really have good evidence after three of the envisaged 25 year rotations have taken place.[22] For the critics of course, by then it will be too late to repair any serious damage!

Barama are complaining that because productivity is low profits are low and they may not expand their operations as planned. There is some talk that the real profitability will come from mineral exploitation in the area rather than from timber exploitation and that the roads constructed for the logging will pave the way for this. Golden Star is already exploring the mineral potential of the area. A separate set of rights is required to actually exploit any mineral deposits discovered and Barama may be interested and use its first refusal rights on mineral exploitation.

At another far smaller concession (45,000 acres) owned by Guyana Timber Industries, situated close to Linden, research is being undertaken on opportunities for market certification of timber products from Guyana.[23] Certification was pioneered in the early 1990s to inform consumers. A number of potential benefits exist. For the company there may be a price premium for certified timber if a market can be identified. Benefits for Guyana include promoting good forest management and demonstrating that the country is moving towards fulfilling international agreements and it could also strengthen international trade. Potential problems with such a system involve higher costs, uncertainties over future market access and demand and the fact that other systems exist to help ensure good forest practices.

For the critics, the weakness of the GFC makes effective monitoring and control very difficult. A further concern is what will be the long term effects of taking out not only highly selective species but also the best specimens on the overall forest ecosystem?

Forest ownership

The Guyana Forestry Commission (GFC), institutionally under the Guyana Natural Resources Agency (GNRA), has responsibility for the 9.1 million ha of declared state forest. Forests outside of designated state forest areas but still on state lands are the responsibility of the Ministry of Agriculture's Lands and Surveys Department. A further area of forest is owned by the local Amerindian community. Designation of the latter area was made on the basis of a survey carried out between 1966 and 1969. Legislation was passed eventually in 1976 designating only a small part of the areas recommended in the survey as Amerindian reserves. The latter include the Mazaruni and NW district, but subsequent mining activity has been intensive in this area. Some of the problems experienced in these areas were discussed when we examined the mining sector. In total about 35,000 Amerindians live in 65 reserves occupying 1.4 million hectares.

Deforestation

Two areas of the country have experienced the most serious deforestation to date. Immediately inland from the coast lie the sandy rolling lands, mainly comprising dry evergreen seasonal forests and savannas. These areas provide the fuelwood, charcoal and much of the timber needs of the 90% of the population who live on the coast. It is estimated that half a million hectares have been denuded here.[24] Fires have been caused by charcoal makers and settlers. The problem is sufficiently serious that CIDA is supporting a research programme into the rehabilitation of the forests in this area. Many of the women living along the coast spend hours every day in the search for fuelwood to cook meals for their families and in some cases for the preparation of animal feed. Collecting fuel and tending the open fire frequently costs many hours of hard labour for women every day.[25] In addition, given that 104,000 ha of sandy rolling lands is estimated to be underlain by bauxite, a further expansion of strip mining will only add to the deforestation.

A second area badly effected is the mangroves, again because of their juxtaposition to the dense coastal population. Most mangrove deforestation has occurred in the past 25 years, significantly worsening coastal erosion, increasing vulnerability to flooding and with as yet unquantified negative effects on fish and crustacean resources and avifauna. The whole issue of the mangroves is central to the issue of coastal zone management and it is important to set out some of the main dimensions of the problem.

There is no coordination of coastal zone management in the country. This lack of coordination at the level of government is no less apparent amongst the donor community as both the EEC and the UNDP through the FAO initiated separate mangrove studies without any coordination of effort. Mangroves protected the whole of the coast up to the mid-17th century.[26] Thereafter the European settlers increasingly altered the coastal zone. The Dutch, delighted to find an environment ripe for their expertise in land reclamation for fertile agricultural production, began the process of building sea defences, dams and dykes. A mud sea wall was constructed behind a mangrove screen to keep out the sea. Dams held water at bay on the landward side. Criss-crossing the enclosed area were irrigation and drainage channels, drained by sluices or kokars in the sea wall. As the tide fell the sluices were opened to allow drainage. Separate irrigation channels are used to bring water back into the fields in dry weather. The enclosed system excluded traditional mangrove coastal zone protection within its boundaries.

Guyana has a coastline extending from the Waini river on the western Venezuela border to the Corentyne river on the Surinam border in the east. According to a recent World Bank study, Guyana's 530 km coastline comprises

225 km of earth dam, 75 km of concrete wall, 5 km of boulders, 9 km of "other defence and 217 km of natural defence".[27] The disappearance of the mangroves in front of the sea defences has made the defences more vulnerable to breaches. This should point an important lesson for future management strategies.

It is clear that there is a real lack of hard scientific data to explain the rapid decline in mangroves beyond increased population pressure on the resource. One hypothesis suggests that in some areas the blocking of drainage channels could be a major factor, as "with the substantial decrease in the flow of fresh water, the sweet-salt water balance was upset resulting in weakening and death of mangrove trees".[28] Mangroves can only tolerate a certain degree of salinity, beyond this they become weakened and vulnerable to wave action. Essentially the mangrove resource has never been taken responsibility for by government. As Hussain's study of the mangroves comments:

> A National Forestry Action Plan ... did not take the mangrove vegetation as a component of the forest resources and therefore, no plan for mangrove vegetation has been included in the formulation of the action plan.[29]

The lesson that emerges from a series of uncoordinated studies of mangroves to date is that the only way to make sense of the problem is through an integrated coastal zone management approach.

The opening up of the forest resource to the outside world poses a threat of widespread deforestation. New road and infrastructure construction programmes will open up additional areas of forest for exploitation as is the case with the road to Brazil. It is not simply the logging operations but also the mining and settlement that the roads might bring that also has an impact. It has been the very inaccessibility of the forests so far that has provided their protection and protected too the livelihoods of the Amerindian communities who depend upon the forests.

National forestry action programme

Guyana formulated a National Forestry Action Programme (NFAP) in 1989. Execution of the plan was the responsibility of the Guyana Natural Resources Agency (GNRA). The main imperative behind this initiative was to massively expand the timber industry. This accounted for a little over 60% of the approximate US$ 90 million budget attached to the "Short Term Action Programme" (STAP). Overall stagnation in the economy constrained forestry activities over the 1970s and 1980s, but the new economic reform programme is seen as an avenue of opportunity to open up the forestry sector.

A key difficulty openly acknowledged by the NFAP is the almost complete absence of qualified personnel, institutional resources, legislation and policy instruments, in addition to the necessary financial resources to enable effective natural resource management. A strength of the NFAP is, therefore, its emphasis on institutional capacity building which accounts for 26% of the proposed budget for the STAP. The stated intention is to set up a system of protected areas, yet the conservation activities only account for 7% of the STAP. The remainder of the STAP budget comprises relatively modest components for "Forestry in Land Use" and "Wood Energy". Although considerable effort was put into the formulation of the NFAP in 1989 there was a three year delay before its presentation to the donor community. The plan had a mixed reception. There were queries raised concerning: the failure to demonstrate how proposed reforestation projects will benefit the coastal poor, who heavily depend on the resource; the lack of local Guyanese participation in the planning process; and an absence of prescriptions concerning how to avoid forest degradation through logging.[30] Amongst the donor community there was a desire to strengthen the conservation components of the NFAP and try to find more innovative ways of harnessing this with the developmental imperative.

There is no doubting from the written intent of the document that a key principle is guaranteeing sustainable yield, the problem remains of how best this can be guaranteed. As Gradwohl and Greenberg explain

> It is possible to exploit tropical forests sustainably, but this usually means keeping to low levels of extraction and to long periods in which the land is left to rest and recover. Techniques which hold promise for the future are usually more expensive in the short term than methods used for the rapid extraction of forest resources.[31]

Quite rightly, countries of the South point to the hypocrisy of the North in its strictures to preserve the tropical forests as global pollution sinks when the North has destroyed its own temperate forests. The sting in the development tail however is that the deforestation of temperate zone forests can create agriculturally productive land use, which is not necessarily the case with the tropical forests. It is now acknowledged that the deforestation that has taken place worldwide incurred an unnecessary degree of soil loss which any wise government would avoid in the future. Duncan Poore's study takes the argument further to state that:

In most other parts of the world, forests can be destroyed but most of the tree species survive; and even many of the other woodland organisms can exist outside the forest or in small fragments of it. This does not seem to be the case in the wet tropics; so exceptional care is needed if it is wished to develop these lands in ways which do not waste their resources.[32]

Even by the late 1990s nothing much had happened with the NFAP concerning funding or staffing.[33] It remains an open question whether this can be revived and put on a proper footing.

Programme for sustainable tropical forestry (PSTF)

President Hoyte of Guyana made an offer at the Commonwealth Heads of Government meeting in October 1989, to set aside 900,000 acres of tropical Amazonian rain forest for an international programme to preserve unique biodiversity and to study the sustainable utilisation of tropical forestry.[34] A project proposal to cover start-up costs was submitted to the Global Environmental Facility and accepted for funding.[35] The aims of this US$ 3.9 million project are:

a) To establish an International Programme Management Group to initiate and develop the overall programme for sustainable tropical forestry;
b) To design and construct a base camp for the Project Site;
c) To collect physical baseline data on the Project Site for a reliable and detailed site profile and to conduct surveys of flora and (avi)fauna;
d) To set up hydro-meteorological stations for the project site; and
e) To develop the institutional framework for the Programme for Sustainable Tropical Forestry, the development of a research programme and the drawing up of a long-term Financing Plan for the overall programme.

The PSTF is intended to include the following, long term:
a) Amazon rainforest wilderness preserve (60% of the area);
b) Sustainable utilisation of tropical forests (40% of the area);
c) International centre for research and training for the sustainable management of tropical rain forests;
d) International environment communications centre.

Having a clearly demarcated area set aside permanently as a forest reserve is absolutely essential. Duncan Poore in his global study for the International Tropical Timber Organisation makes absolutely clear that the first priority of sustainable production is long-term security.[36] There can be no sustainability unless the forest is secured.

A number of concerns arise with this project. The first is the means by which the area will be protected in practice. The new road to Lethem and Brazil will both ease access to the site but increase encroachment pressures. It is quite possible that immigrants from Brazil will arrive in numbers if the Guyanese economy begins to take off. Measures must be taken to mitigate the possible effects on the site of the road and the attendant developments. On the positive side, prices of goods for the inhabitants of the interior will be reduced, as will the heavy cost of human transportation.

A further concern is the relationship between the proposed international institutes and the process of institution building nationally. Clearly it is in Guyana's interests to get the best national value added possible for institution building and human resource development from the STAP initiative. Having an expensive international institute isolated from the national context of institution building would clearly not be in the best interests of the country. It could also consume a dis-proportionate share of the project budget. However, the attraction of an international institute is also apparent. It can bring in further support and promulgate to the World, through easy international scientific and media access, both the progress and the problems that the initiative is encountering.

Tropenbos

The Tropenbos project funded by the Dutch government is researching the sustainability of tropical forest resource exploitation and comprises a series of sub-projects. A field research station has been established at Mabura Hills Reserve. Tropenbos works with the University of Guyana (UG) on the project. As a matter of principle it is important to link up all such external initiatives with a local institutional base in order to maximise human resource development and institutional capacity building. The level of UG participation both in the Tropenbos initiative and in other similar initiatives on aspects of sustainable resource management must be made a priority. A regular newsletter is produced by Tropenbos.[37]

Throughout the 1990s Tropenbos has made a valuable and extensive contribution to knowledge about the management of the country's tropical forests. A series of research publications have appeared on a whole range of issues.[38] One of the most interesting findings was the rediscovery of a wide

38

ranging national forest inventory undertaken in the late 1960s with UNDP and FAO support, which lay gathering dust on the GFC shelves.[39] The data was transformed from its original user-unfriendly handwritten format into digital form.

There are still barriers to overcome with the Tropenbos programme, notably the strengthening of local institutions and capacity and the fact that they have not as yet been able to translate the detailed scientific results into a full and operational management system. However ten major conclusions have emerged from their work thus far.[40]:

1. Forestry using low intensity exploitation is the best land use for sandy soils.
2. Such low intensity logging (20 to 25 cubic meters per hectare) on sandy soils appears to have little adverse impact on hydrology and the nutrient cycle.
3. A non-logged buffer strip must be maintained along creeks and on steep slopes to avoid erosion and siltation.
4. Greenheart forests cannot sustain a second harvest after 20-25 years.
5. Silviculture treatments are necessary following harvesting to compensate for low growth rates and a decline in the population of commercial species.
6. Uncontrolled skidding creates serious damage to the ecosystem.
7. Directional (herringbone) felling should be used to reduce the impact of skidding.
8. Gaps in the canopy should be kept small.
9. Gaps should be as evenly spaced as possible.
10. Gap size will influence the future species composition of the forest.

Effects of forestry on biodiversity

The globally unique biodiversity wealth of Guyana is inextricably tied up with its forest areas. The extent to which the logging industry is developed and the way in which the logging occurs are absolutely crucial considerations in maintaining the potential developmental wealth tied up over the long term with this currently undervalued asset. Only the timber resource is currently being utilised within the forests and this represents a lost development opportunity. There is a small trade in wildlife, much of it not through official channels. Eco-tourism is only now beginning to develop and the role of the forests here will be essential.

Essential safeguards

The essential safeguards for sustainable forestry are:

1) Undertake an accurate inventorisation of Guyana's forests.
2) Delineate clearly forest areas by type of usage, namely national parks and reserves which exclude commercial logging, mining and other environmentally destructive activity; areas for sustainable commercial logging; lands belonging to the Amerindian community; special protection for mangroves is required as an integral component of a coastal management programme. Ensure long term consistency of usage by classification, in particular for land belonging to the Amerindian community and for national parks and reserves.
3) In the areas delineated for commercial logging establish sustainable yields for the various forest types and zones. Ensure that these are written into all logging agreements.
4) Establish adequate monitoring and enforcement procedures.

Notes

1. *National Forestry Action Plan 1990-2000,* Guyana Forestry Commission and Canadian International Development Agency, 1989.

2. GAHEF, *Development Trends and Environmental Impacts in Guyana*, National Report to the UNCED Conference, 1992. Note that this report draws heavily on the earlier work of Melville Gajraj, *Development Trends and Environmental Impacts in Guyana*, February 1991.

3. UNDP, *GEF Assistance to the Programme for Sustainable Tropical Forestry Project Document*, No GUY/91/A/99, 1991.

4. World Bank (1991), *op.cit*, p.15.

5. UNDP, *GEF Project Document, op.cit*, p.4.

6. EIU, *Guyana Country Report No 3*, 1991, p.33.

7. *The Guardian*, 1 November 1991.

8.   *Starbroek News*, 9 March 1993.

9.   *Mirror,* 7 March 1993.

10. *Catholic Standard*, 21 March 1993.

11. See Tropenbos, *The Tropenbos Programme Information Series 1,* Tropenbos Foundation, 1989.

12. Interview with Mr Bauer, Tropenbos Researcher, Georgetown, Guyana, 14 January 1991.

13. Investment contract between Government of Guyana and Sunkyond Ltd of Korea, Sampling Corporation SDN, BHD of Malaysia and Barama Co Ltd of Guyana (note the following information is taken from the text of the contract).

14. *Catholic Standard*, 21 February 1993.

15. *Starbroek News*, 20 February 1993.

16. *Starbroek News,* 9 March 1993.

17. *Catholic Standard,* 14 May 1993.

18. *ibid.*

19. *ibid.*

20. G. Sutton, *Barama Company Project, Northwest Guyana*, a paper given at the conference on Environment and Development in Guyana, Centre for Developing Areas Research, Royal Holloway, University of London, 7 May 1997.

21. *ibid.*

22. *ibid.*

23. A. Parasam, *Market certification of timber products from Guyana*, a paper given at the conference on Environment and Development in

Guyana, Centre for Developing Areas Research, Royal Holloway, University of London, 7 May 1997.

24.   *National Forestry Action Plan, op.cit.*

25.   See "The Life of Ione Halley, Guyana" in I. Dankelman and J. Davidson (eds), *Women and Environment in the Third World*, Earthscan, London, 1988, pp.83-85.

26.   See V.C. Lakham, "Planning and Development Experiences in the Coastal Zone of Guyana" in *Ocean and Coastal Management* 22, 1993, pp.169-186 and R.B. Latchmansingh, "Sea Defence Construction in Guyana, Models Adopted Difficulties Experienced" (internal document) Caribbean Engineering and Management Consultants, Georgetown, 1995. However one author puts the time somewhat earlier, in the early 17th century, see H.G. Dalton, *The Short History of British Guyana*, Longman Brown, Green and Longmans, London, 1955.

27.   World Bank, *Guyana: Public Sector Review*, Washington DC, World Bank, 1993. A considerably different set of figures are produced in a slightly earlier FAO report, see M.Z. Hussian, *Restoration and Expansion of the Mangrove Belt in Guyana*, a report prepared for the Hydraulics Division of the Ministry of Agriculture by the FAO, Rome, May 1990, p.5.

28.   *ibid*, p.10.

29.   *ibid*, p.12.

30.   M. Colchester and L. Lohmann, *The Tropical Forestry Action Plan: What Progress?* World Rainforest Movement and the Ecologist, 1990, pp.23-29.

31.   J. Gradwohl and R. Greenberg, *Saving the Tropical Forests*, Earthscan, London, 1988, p.51.

32.   D. Poore, *No Timber without Trees: Sustainability in the Tropical Forest,* Earthscan, London, 1989, p.2.

33.   Personal communication, Patrick Williams, UNDP Guyana, 7 May 1997.

34. See Commonwealth-Government of Guyana, *Programme for Sustainable Tropical Forestry*, Commonwealth Secretariat, London, August 1990.

35. See UNDP (1991), *op.cit.*

36. D. Poore (1989), *op.cit*, p.197.

37. *Kykoveral Newsletter*, Utrecht.

38. Tropenbos publications include: *Checklist of Woody Plants of Guyana (1988); A Monograph of Wallaba, Mora and Greenheart (1990); Major Timber Trees of Guyana: A Field Guide (1992); Patterns in Tropical Rain Forest in Guyana (1992); Hemiphot: A Programme to Analyze Vegetation Indices, Light and Light Quality from Hemispherical Photographs (1994); Modelling the Effects of Logging on the Water Balance of a Tropical Rain Forest (1993); SOAP-Soil Atmosphere Plant Model (1994); Growth and Survival of Tropical Rain Forest Tree Seedlings in Forest Understorey and Canopy Openings (1994); Major Timber Trees of Guyana: A Lens Key (1994); Growth of Tropical Rain Forest Trees as Dependent on Phosphorus Supply (1994); Ecology and Logging in a Tropical Rain Forest in Guyana (1996); Major Timber Trees of Guyana: Timber Characteristics and Utilization (1996).*

39. "Sustainable Forest Management: Tropenbos' role", *Guyana Review* No 44, September 1996.

40. *ibid.*

4 Agriculture and fishing

Agriculture

Agriculture has traditionally been the mainstay of the economy. It accounted for 25.9% of GDP in 1985 but by 1990 this had declined to 23.5%.[1] Privatisation initiatives led to a significant rallying of output in the 1990s with production of the two main crops growing from 132,000 tons to 253,000 tons in the case of sugar over the 1990 to 1994 period and in the case of rice from 93,400 tones to 233, 000 tons over the same period.[2] The sector as a whole employs over 35% of the labour force and provides most of the domestic food supply.[3] The vast majority of agricultural production occurs on the wet clays of the coastal plain. The country receives plenty of seasonal rainfall, the problem is ensuring sufficient drainage during the rainy season and irrigation in the dry season. It relies heavily on a complex system of land use management. The establishment and management of water conservancies on the coastal plain has been vital in this regard. Agriculture is also dependent upon effective sea defences and the complex system of drainage and irrigation.

Historically sugar has been the mainstay of the economy, to such an extent that it has determined the settlement pattern in Guyana. Initially, in the 17th and 18th centuries, settlers attempted to establish coffee and cotton plantations in the interior, but poor soil quality soon led to failure. Later sugar was tried along the coastal strip. By 1820 this was firmly established as the country's main crop and has remained so ever since, worked first by slave labour from Africa, until slavery's abolition in 1834 then subsequently by indentured labour from India but also including Chinese and Portuguese labour. Sugar production along the coast thus determined the highly distorted pattern of human settlement, which developed where the jobs were. In 1992 sugar still accounted for over half of all agricultural production. The sugar industry was run by two companies, Booker Brothers McConnell and Co and Jessel Securities. Both were nationalised in the mid-1970s and were subsequently run by the Guyana Sugar Corporation (GUYSUCO). Nationalisation led to a sharp decline in sugar production, which fell to 132,000 tons in 1990, representing only 37% of production prior to nationalisation. For three consecutive years to 1990 GUYSUCO was even unable to meet Guyana's sugar quota allocations from the EU and the US. From October 1990 the government invited in Booker and Tate and Lyle to assume management of the sector. The upturn was immediate. In 1991 production rose to 162,600 tons and in 1992 rocketed up to 247,000 tons.[4] The investment famine associated with Guyana's socialist experiment combined with the inept implementation of nationalisation meant that the whole drainage system required a drastic overhaul to improve production. Immediate requirements included equipment for drainage maintenance, and large pumps for draining areas where temporary earth dams were erected at breaches in the sea defences.

Rice, the second most important crop, accounting for 7% of overall agricultural production in 1992, is used both for export and domestic consumption. Approximately 15,000 farmers produce paddy. Rice is grown both by small and by large scale farmers along the coastal strip. Again production declined dramatically from 183,200 tons in 1986 to 93,400 tons in 1990 (a particularly bad year as heavy rain prevented harvesting).[5] Many farmers stopped producing rice and abandoned fields or switched to food production for the local market. The monopoly role of the Guyana Rice Board has been blamed for many of the problems in the industry.[6] Rice production increased two and a half times over the period 1990 to 1994. There were various reasons. 1990 had been a particularly bad year because of erratic and unusual rainfall but more positively production levels responded to the freeing up of prices, rice planting increased as growers responded to the new macroeconomic and political dispensation.

The situation in the two largest agricultural land development schemes, Black Bush Polder and Mahaica Mahaicony Abary, illustrated the difficulties, with poor feeder roads, silted drainage and irrigation channels, many inoperable pumping stations and abandoned storage facilities, with breaches in the sea defences and eroded conservancy dams.

The main problem of the agricultural sector in Guyana is not essentially one of land hunger, as only 1% of the territory is cultivated. People are said to have been abandoning the land and moving to the urban centres mainly because insufficient attention was given in the past to provide the necessary package of support to make farming worthwhile. Yet existing statistics on rates of urbanisation remain modest, at 1.3% according to Thomas.[7] Some of the rural drift will be accounted for by emigration, with the annual rate for 1992 being 0.7%.[8] In addition to inadequate irrigation and drainage there were no price incentives and limited access to markets. Rice lands were also lost because of the fragility of sea defences. For example, 400 hectares were lost from Lusignan Island in 1989.[9] For non-traditional crops the spoilage rate was extremely high, up to 60%. With government now providing better incentives for farming this should slow down urban drift and thereby reduce growing pressures on the urban environment as a long term concern.

For Mark Pelling, whilst a decline in environmental management infrastructure may indeed reduce livelihood opportunities there is a hidden subsidy via the extensive levels of remittances from overseas which support a considerable number of household incomes.[10] Hence, it may be the case that rural infrastructural decline has promulgated a great flexibility in livelihood strategies rather than an extensive rural-urban migration.

Livestock has had mixed fortunes. Whilst beef production increased from 2,100,000 tons in 1988 to 3,840,ooo tons in 1993, poultry production remained static and pork and eggs decline.[11] More significant was the decline in milk yields as the Burnham government had imported Cuban Holstein-Zebu cattle in 1984 to improve milk yields but these fell from 4.22 m litres in 1988 to 0.850 m litres in 1994.[12]

Renewing the water management system

There are urgent and multiple challenges for the agricultural sector. These relate both to the needs of the agricultural sector itself and because the whole land use system of the densely populated coastal zone is constructed around the network of dykes which are everyone's front yard in Guyana. Of prime importance is the task of restoring the coastal defences, the drainage and irrigation systems. Studies compiled at the beginning of the 1990s suggested that improved water management practices could increase sugar and rice yields by 20% and ground provisions by 40%.[13] Much would depend upon whether such initiatives could be carried out in an environmentally sensitive manner. Possible effects on other users of the system need to be taken into account. As agricultural production is reinvigorated along the coast, this may have a further negative effect on the mangroves as a result of the new work on sea defences and drainage. Care needs to be taken to avoid this happening.

Whilst efforts are being made to manage the conservancies this has not been the case for the watersheds which supply the conservancies. The Sandy Rolling Plain, known locally as the "Sand Hills" backing the coastal plain, provides the watersheds for the agricultural areas but there are potentially multiple conflicts over natural resource use, as a number of sectors operate here. Extensive bauxite mining has led to large scale deforestation. Land clearance for agricultural production and demand for fuelwood have also played their part in deforestation. Maintaining the forest cover is important to ensure infiltration of rainwater into the ground and the recharging of aquifers. Deforestation impedes this creating erosion and flash flooding. Ensuring successful long term agricultural production will require improving watershed management as a future concern.

Chemical inputs

The heavy agricultural chemical inputs of fertilizers, pesticides, etc. is of major concern. There is evidence that chemicals are used in an indiscriminate manner. The extent of the misuse is difficult to quantify as there is no monitoring of pesticide residues in crops, animals or water.[14] If projected future levels of rice and sugar production are to be realised, this will signify a massive increase in the application of chemicals to the land. As agricultural production is based on drainage and irrigation systems this inevitably means that there will also be an impact on the people who live in the coastal area. This will result both from aerial spraying and from chemical inputs, which can accumulate in fields, especially rice paddy, before entering into the water channels which pass in front of human settlements, as this common water resource is used for domestic needs. As the *Guyana Review* reports: "The increased use of fertilisers and pesticides - which facilitated the increased rice production - is likely to have reduced the quality of freshwater supply along the coast. Actually it is estimated that 90% of pesticides applied to the rice crops for the "blast" disease do not reach the pest, but are likely either to be washed into waterways or dispersed in the atmosphere."[15] Water from the canals also carries pollution from inland mining operations in addition to coastal agricultural and industrial activity. The problem is that it is also used for domestic purposes, bathing, washing clothes, a play area, etc. It is not for nothing that Georgetown is known as the Venice of Latin America.

Kayman Sankar Ltd are responsible for more than a third of the country's rice production and the management is well aware of the potential problems associated with the high level of chemical application and therefore invited the government early on, to help them cope better with the problems.[16] Conditions were probably better here than in most other locations. Still the situation in early 1992 was one in which all the chemicals were stored together in a hut without adequate ventilation and with seepage from a number of barrels which produced a heady gaseous cocktail when the store room was opened. The chemicals store was sited too close to the main factory with inadequate precautions around the storage site. Empty petro chemical drums were dumped on flat land not far from the main processing site, both near water courses and the milling residues. In spite of management rules that workers handling chemicals wear masks, during field operations this is honoured in the breach, i.e. most ignore it. Water from the canals is used to wash out the chemical components used in the aerial spraying. Neighbouring residents have complained that inadequate warning is given of spraying times and that there is harmful chemical drift. A GAHEF monitoring trip was unable to confirm the latter complaint made by local people but wind conditions vary on a daily basis. This particular company appeared keen to improve its practices and invited the government's environment agency to give educational talks to its workers and management. This raises the important issue of the need to strengthen institutional capacity to be able to deliver the support requested by industry.

The agricultural chemicals which eventually are washed out to sea may seriously affect spawning grounds and coastal flora and fauna and may be a contributory factor to the decline in the shrimp catch in recent years. We turn next to examine the fishing sector.

Fishing

Fishing has traditionally played an important role in the economic life of the predominantly coastal population. Fish provide an estimated 40% of the animal protein consumed and furnish approximately 5% of export earnings. The coastal waters are rich in nutrients, which account for the good fishing, mainly as a result of silt deposited by the Amazon river in Brazil.[17] The local rivers are rich in tannin. Fishing is carried out along the continental shelf. This extends to 175 km at its widest point in the east of the country and narrows to 100 km in the west whilst the depth varies between 2 and 200 metres. Freshwater rivers, lakes and irrigation channels provide a further small input to the industry, both as a source of local food and of ornamental fish for export, very much a minor trade.

Marine fisheries includes both industrial and artesanal sub-sectors. Artesanal fishing is by far the most important of the two, accounting for almost 80% of the estimated total catch of marine and freshwater fish.[18] There were 1,171 vessels in this sub-sector, employing 4,000 fisherman, many organised into cooperative societies at the beginning of the 1990s. There were 128 trawlers in the industrial sector along with three shrimp and fish processing plants. Shrimp are an important resource.[19] Over half of the trawlers are foreign owned and they concentrate in the main on prawns for export. Before the introduction of the 200 mile territorial limit at sea, foreign fleets used to follow the tuna and shrimp along the whole north west coast of Latin America plundering the stocks. It is generally agreed that the intensity of fishing was excessive at that time.

Fish resources beyond the continental shelf are unquantified. Scientific estimates of the fish resource on the shelf itself are only known as a result of a study carried out by the Norwegians in 1988.[20] The study found that the total catch of fin-fish stocks had rapidly increased from 30,000 tonnes in 1980 to about 40,000 tonnes during 1984-87. The report warns "the estimate of the potential long term yield is 45,000 tonnes. This is a rough indication that most of the fin-fish stocks are fully utilised".[21] Further evidence of a growing pressure on the resource base was the finding that the density of biomass is markedly lower in Guyana then in neighbouring Surinam, which may be a result of the higher rate of exploitation.

The main pressure at present is upon the prawn resource and soon it will be upon the shrimp bob also. The prawn catch has been in steady decline. In 1980 the whole weight catch was 6,851 tons and this fell to under 2,000 tons in 1989. The sustainable catch of prawns is now generally accepted to have been exceeded. A management plan was devised to ban prawn fishing between November and January each year but was never introduced. However, as an absolute minimum level of response to this crisis situation no new shrimp trawlers were allowed to enter the industry in the early 1990s and any trawler that left the industry could not be replaced.

A major difficulty lies in obtaining reliable estimates of the catch and this is tied up with the way the industry is organised. Companies commission the captains and their crew to shrimp. They are then paid a percentage of the catch that is landed. Hence it is in the interests of the captain to try to sell most of his catch before it is landed to boats that liaise illegally at sea at agreed times. The captains have an informal agreement between themselves as to the levels of catch they will bring in. The captain then cuts a deal with the crew. Thus finding out the real weight of catches has been an impossible exercise. The recorded figures are always within a suspiciously narrow range, in spite of the wide diversity that might be expected by the natural vagaries of the catch.

The fisheries department has been severely handicapped for a long period of time in monitoring the catches, by having no boats and limited human and financial resources. Officers were obliged to travel in the fishing fleet boats if they do go out and either through fear or because they receive a share of the profit they may become privy to the vow of silence. The Fisheries Department therefore has had to rely on catch and effort information in the past which at best is only about 60% accurate. The coastguard service now has a boat, but before the 1990s only occasionally were foreign fishing boats apprehended for fishing red snapper within the 200 mile limit. As the 1990s progressed arrests were announced in the press on a more regular basis on Venezuelan, Trinidadian, Surinamese and Guyanese vessels.

What all of this means is that establishing and monitoring sustainable fishing limits is very difficult. The evidence shows that the limits are being reached and beyond. With no resources, the possibility of government instituting any effective controls, such as protecting nursery areas, has not been a viable option to date.

A number of possible reasons have been put forward for the decline in the shrimp catch beyond overfishing. Research is required to determine the source of the problem. What is happening to the juveniles? Is the use of Chinese seine and pin seine nets largely to blame for their destruction or is it because the mangroves are being destroyed and therefore the nursery sites? Is it to do with changes in river run-off as a result of economic activities inland with mining, industrial and agricultural chemicals entering the rivers and water channels or is it due to changes in rainfall or even to changes in the coast? These questions all pose the challenge of the need to improve intersectoral coordination through effective coastal zone management. We shall return to these issues later in greater detail.

In the 1980s there was a terribly wasteful practice of throwing the "by-catch" brought up with the shrimp fishing back into the ocean. With the liberalisation measures in the 1990s the boats are now willingly bringing in the "by-catch" to sell and are looking after it better as they can now realise a profit on the operation.

There is growing concern about the disappearance of a number of once common freshwater fish caught along the coast, including the houri, sunfish, patwa and hassa.[22] These are now only found further inland. The precise reason for this is not known. But agricultural, mining, industrial and urban waste pollution entering the water system untreated, probably plays a role here. Aquaculture exists on a small localised scale. Any future expansion of activities will need to take care to minimise both mangrove destruction and over intensive fishing. There is also a small ornamental fish trade on the upper reaches of rivers.

Notes

1.   EIU, *Guyana Country Profile 1991-92*, *op.cit*, p.13.

2.   EIU, *Guyana Country Profile 1995-96*, p.17.

3.   World Bank (1991), *op.cit*, p.11.

4.   EIU, *Guyana Country Profile 1993-94*, p.13.

5.   *ibid.*

6.   C. Singh, *Guyana: Politics in a Plantation Society*, Praeger, New York, 1988, p.112.

7. C.Y. Thomas, *Social Development and the Social Summit: A Look at Guyana, Jamaica and Trinidad and Tobago*, IDS, University of Guyana, Georgetown, 1995.

8. Bureau of Statistics, *Guyana Statistical Bulletin*, Vol 4, No 1, Bureau of Statistics, Georgetown, 1995.

9. FAO *Restoration and Expansion of the Mangrove Belt in Guyana*, TCP/GUY/8953, FAO, Rome, 1990.

10. Personal communication from Mark Pelling who is completing his doctoral thesis on Guyana at the University of Liverpool.

11. EIU, *Guyana Country Profile 1995-96*, p.18.

12. *ibid.*

13. World Bank (1991), *op.cit*, p.13.

14. GAHEF, *Developing Trends and Environmental Impacts in Guyana*, National Report to the UNCED Conference, 1992.

15. *Guyana Review*, No 47, December 1996, p.30.

16. Field visit to Kayman Sankar estates and rice mill on the Essequibo coast, 13 January 1992.

17. M. Hanif, *An overview of the natural resources of Guyana*, Institute of Applied Science and Technology, 1988, and C.L. Abernethy, *Recommendations for a Future Sea Defence Strategy*, Hydraulics Research Station, Wallingford, 1980.

18. This figure is calculated from data provided in GAHEF, *Development Trends and Environmental Impacts in Guyana*, 1991, p.34.

19. L. Villegas and A. Dragovich, "The Guianas-Brazil Shrimp Industry" in J.A. Gullard and B.J. Rothschild, *Penaid Shrimp: Their Biology and Management*, US Department of Commerce, Miami, 1984, pp.60-70.

20.   Institute of Marine Research, *Surveys of the Fish Resources in the Shelf Areas between Surinam and Columbia 1988*, a study carried out under the NORAD/UNDP/FAO programme, Bergen, 1988.

21.   *ibid*, p.58.

22.   Interview with Mr Rubin Charles, Chief Fisheries Officer, Ministry of Agriculture, Georgetown, 8 February 1992.

5 Human settlement and service provision

Housing and overcrowding

Accurate statistics on human settlement are impossible to come by but the essential problems are known. Nine out of every ten people, in a population of 800,000, live along the coast. Up to a quarter and a third of the total population may live in the capital city Georgetown.[1] Once known as the Venice of the Caribbean, Georgetown experienced a gradual deterioration in the 1970s and 1980s, a situation which is widely acknowledged and lamented by the inhabitants. What was once highly regarded as the "Garden City" is now derided by the inhabitants as the "Garbage City"!

The capital city in particular suffers from an acute housing shortage and the growth of unplanned squatter settlements from the late 1980s, but so too do the other main towns of Linden, New Amsterdam, Rose Hall and Corriverton. Linda Peake has characterised the situation in stark terms, "Overcrowding, insecure shelter and increasing levels of homelessness are the primary characteristics of the housing situation in Guyana in the early 1990s."[2] Many of those in salaried employment in the state and private sector are affected, not only the poor. Many of those Agricultural and rural neglect may have contributed towards increasing urbanisation and a growing pressure on every aspect of urban service provision, including housing, water supply, sewage, solid waste disposal, energy supply and transportation. The current situation across all of these sectors is unacceptable.

There is a growing housing shortage in urban areas and a deterioration of the existing housing stock, with the exception of the more well off inhabitants. One set of statistics available suggested that by the mid-1980s there was a total deficit of 32,000 units of housing out of approximately 167,000 households, or about 20% of the total, with estimates suggesting that 7,000 new housing units would have to be constructed per year just to catch up with housing requirements by the year 2000.[3] Using data collected later in 1991, immediate housing need was calculated as 33,641 units nationally, with 30% of need located in Georgetown.[4] Up until the mid-1990s the government was not involved in any significant housing construction and in the absence of an urban land policy, people have taken to squatting and unplanned settlement. This has been the case generally in areas of urban settlement but it is also the case in rural areas. Limited efforts have been made to regularise squatting and to privatise the public housing stock. Inevitably squatter settlements lack even a bare minimum of service provision. As long ago as 1971 the National Nutrition and Food Survey estimated 3 to 4 people slept to a room amongst low income groups and the most recent reports suggest the figure is considerably higher in the 1990s.[5] A report by the Government of Guyana and the Inter American Development Bank revealed that 60% of households in Georgetown had other persons living with them.[6]

Crowded and cramped conditions facilitate the spread of tuberculosis, meningitis, influenza and other diseases, especially if people are poorly fed. Household accidents increase, not least because houses are constructed on inappropriate sites. There are greater social tensions within the family or living group given decreasing personal space within living units, with higher levels of domestic violence against women and children.[7]

Service provision

Water provision is an essential prerequisite for urban living. In terms of quantitative water provision, official statistics state that over 90% of the urban and 75% of the rural population has access to piped water. But provision of water has declined in both a qualitative and quantitative sense. Indeed provision of potable water has declined to such an extent that by the late 1980s only 40% of water samples met WHO bacteriological standards.[8] It is little wonder therefore that diarrhoeal diseases figure prominently and these are particularly dangerous for children. Each year the country experiences mini-epidemics of typhoid and gastroenteritis and the response is to encourage citizens to boil all drinking waters, as the "Guyana Review" notes, "The problem is seldom dealt with at its source." [9] Growing squatter settlements near the water provisioning systems have undoubtedly contributed to deteriorating water quality. In Georgetown in particular, extensive squatting around the Lamaha Canal poses grave dangers to the city's main water supply. There are added fears in this regard given recent cholera epidemics in neighbouring countries.

As Cairncross has pointed out, emphasis is always mistakenly given to water quality rather than the importance of water quantity as a means of improving health.[10] Lack of adequate water leads to poor hygiene and increased risk of disease, in particular diarrhoeal disease and infectious skin diseases.

In the capital city water losses are estimated at 55% with impure water contaminating the supply through broken pipes.[11] In the main, the city's water supply comes from the Larna Conservancy, whilst wells are the primary water source for the suburbs and rural areas, in addition to river water in the interior. In the rural areas, it is estimated that seven out of ten people do not receive a regular water supply, hence the vast numbers of people seen carrying water by one means or another along the country roads. Lack of maintenance and spares mean many wells are inoperative. The panoply of problems in the sector include streamlining water administration whilst building human resource and institutional capacity, revenue collection and investment.

Georgetown has a sewerage system with 12,000 connections. All sewage is pumped untreated into the Demerara river. Elsewhere pit latrines are used in rural areas and septic tanks in other urban centres. Most are poorly built and maintained which coupled with a high water table and periodic flooding makes them a health risk. Industrial effluent and nutrient enrichment because of fertiliser run-off has led to the canals becoming blocked with weeds.[12]

Solid waste management has been in long term decline. Collection is infrequent given administrative, financial and mechanical difficulties within municipal authorities. As a result, waste lies uncollected being both a health and fire hazard or is disposed of into the canals thereby worsening drainage and sanitation problems. The minimum waste deficit in Georgetown is estimated to be 28,000 cubic yards per year.[13] The system of using the canals to clear the waste by washing it out to sea only contributes to coastal pollution with inevitable negative effects on the fishing industry. In urban areas community dumping sites have been established but there is no satisfactory management of these.

A draft master plan for Georgetown's water supply, sewerage and drainage was produced in 1994.[14] Improving garbage collection will lead in turn to improved drainage and less water pollution. It is important that an integrated approach be adopted. In neighbouring Brazil a system of low-cost garbage collection and disposal has been developed in Recife. The aim is to combine goals of employment creation, reducing transport costs, some cost recovery through selling recycled materials and organic compost and in general move towards a more decentralised and appropriate technology solution.[15] Exploring the possibilities of developing such a scheme to Guyana could be worthwhile.

Mark Pelling has demonstrated that access to affordable housing, adequate health care and education and economic resources and community development are key factors in the production of household vulnerability to urban flood hazard in Greater Georgetown, an ever present threat.[16] Human settlement and service provision combined with the essentials of health and education in the context of sustainable economic development provides the key to a more secure future.

Notes

1. Economist Intelligence Unit, *Guyana. Country Profile 1995-96*, EIU, 1996, p.12.

2. L. Peake "From co-operative socialism to a social housing policy? Declines and revivals in housing policy in Guyana" in P. Potter and D. Conway (eds), *Housing in the Caribbean*, Indiana UP, Bloomington, 1996.

3. Gajray (1991) *op.cit*, p.15.

4. Central Housing and Planning Authority, *Government of Guyana Housing Policy*, CHPA, Georgetown, 1993.

5. GAHEF (1991), UNCED Report, *op.cit*, p.47.

6. Government of Guyana and Inter American Development Bank, *Urban Rehabilitation Programme. Draft report on condition of physical components*, Government of Guyana, Georgetown, 1993.

7. Peake (1996), *op.cit*.

8. GAHEF (1991), UNCED Report, *op.cit*, p.48.

9. *Guyana Review*, No 47, December 1996, p.30.

10. S. Cairncross "Water supply and the urban poor" in J.E. Hardoy, S. Cairncross and D. Satterthwaite (eds), *The poor die young: Housing and health in Third World Cities*, Earthscan, London, 1990, Chapter 5.

11. World Bank (1991), *op.cit*, p.22.

12. P. Williams (1997) *op.cit*.

13. GAHEF (1991), UNCED report, *op.cit*, p.22.

14. Halcrow plc, *Draft Georgetown Water and Sewerage Master Plan,* Halcrow plc, Swindon, 1994.

15. S. de Coura Cuentro and D.M. Gadji, "The collection and management of household garbage, in J.E. Hardoy *et al* (1990), *op.cit*, Chapter 8.

16. M. Pelling "What determines vulnerability to floods: a case study in Georgetown Guyana" in *Environment and Urbanisation*, April 1997.

6 Industry, transport and energy

Industry

Manufacturing accounts for about 4% of registered GDP.[1] The country has scattered small industries along the coast which means industrial waste is concentrated in specific areas. All waste eventually goes into the water sources. The low level of economic development in the country means industrial pollution is limited. Sugar is the largest food processing industry, but over the 1980s production virtually halved. Following the harvesting of the cane it is ground. The production process uses an astonishing 6,291 gallons of water for every ton of sugar produced, with all of the wastewater entering the drainage canals. At harvest time the canals become anaerobic giving off offensive smells. Some productive recycling of waste occurs within the industry through the production of filter cake as a fertilizer and bagasse to fuel the industry's boilers. With the sugar industry taking off in the late 1990s, care will need to be exercised to minimize future negative environmental effects.

It is undoubtedly the distilleries who are the major source of industrial water pollution in Georgetown, through the discharge of untreated effluent creating noxious odours. Pollution in the rest of the industrial sector is restricted to a few plants producing textiles, electrical appliances, edible oil and soap, a tannery and garages. As the economy continues to grow, a level of industrial expansion will take place. Health and safety in the workplace is clearly a very important issue which deserves increased attention along with a satisfactory Environment Impact Assessment of any new major industrial transport or energy initiative.

Transport

Only a fifth of the country's 1,467 mile road network (figure for the early 1990s) is in good condition, which means increased travel time and high vehicle operating costs. Ferry services are in need of an overhaul along with the floating bridge across the Demerara river. The European Union funded Guyana-

58

Suriname ferry project begun in 1995 was scheduled for completion in 1997.[2] Port facilities are generally in a poor condition. Travel to the interior relies heavily on air transport.

Air pollution as a result of vehicle emissions is not a major environmental problem given the limited number of vehicles in the country. Most of the roads are along the coast with hardly any into the interior. The very lack of transport infrastructure throughout the country is a main reason why so much of the natural environment has remained in tact. The major new development is trying to complete the Georgetown to Letham road on the Brazilian border. There is already a road link from the coast to Mabura Hill. The final link from there to Letham stretches 346 kms and construction began in 1990. The work involves clearing a 50 metre wide stretch of road. Hence in total this means a considerable land clearance exercise. The section from Letham to Kurukupari was completed in 1993 but the link between Mabura Hill and Kurukupari was not even begun by mid-1996.

Negative environmental consequences of the road to Brazil may be substantial and include the possible spread of foot and mouth disease which exists on the Brazilian side of the border but not in Guyana. The road could open up the area to massive population settlement from the Brazil side. Most of the road is flat, which is expected to restrict erosion problems. Probably the most environmentally sensitive stretch goes from Mabura Hill to Kurupukari through the white sand ecosystem, as deforestation here results in rapid depletion of soil nutrients. Road construction for the new forest logging concessions in different parts of the country will have significant environmental impact according to the experts.[3]

Improving transportation within the country is necessary if economic development is to proceed. What is certain is that an extensive programme of road construction in the future would have a serious impact on the environment. In particular this would occur because whole new areas of the country would be opened up to logging, mining and possibly to agricultural production. For this reason it is important to undertake proper Environmental Impact Assessments and to act on the results. At present government institutions responsible for environmental monitoring and control are greatly constrained in fulfilling their role by the expense involved in hiring planes to fly to the interior to check on mining and timber operations. For the future, much depends upon the new Environment Protection Agency and its operational effectiveness.

Energy

In a review of renewable and fossil fuels endowment and potentially exploitable resources for sustained energy production in the Caribbean group of countries, Denis Minott produced a ranking system running from 'not significant' to "major source" for fifteen energy sources.[4] Compared with its Caribbean neighbours Guyana came out as being very well endowed with renewable energy sources. However, Guyana has no commercial quantities of oil or coal resources known at present. The high cost of importing petroleum products has been a heavy burden on the economy since the oil price rises of the early 1970s. In an agreement reached with Venezuela in 1986, oil was to be exchanged for Guyana's bauxite.

The country has enormous hydropower potential. Thus far cost factors have impeded any significant developments, not least because the demand is at the coast whereas potential hydropower sites exist much further inland. In addition, as experiences in Latin America and elsewhere suggest, any hydroelectric scheme must be very carefully evaluated for its environmental and human impacts. As one author has commented "The history of hydroelectric dams in tropical rainforests has not been a happy one."[5] In neighbouring Surinam, according to the same author, the Lake Brokopondo scheme was completed in 1964. The tree decomposition, as the dam filled up, produced noxious hydrogen sulphide gases and complaints of a bad odour. The decomposition turned the water more acidic, corroding the expensive cooling system in the dam, which necessitated added costs. Later the Lake became carpeted with water hyacinth which impedes transportation, clogs machinery and when left on the banks impedes access and gives off a bad smell. These same problems recurred at the Curua Una dam in Brazil. Malaria and schistosomiasis diseases can spread. Fish can die downstream due to anaerobic decomposition as occurred at Brokopondo. Such large schemes lead to a waste of forest resources which are drowned by the formation of lakes and the displacement of indigenous peoples whose homes might have been in the area for centuries. When the dam building coincides with extensive gold mining, as in many areas of Brazil, this can increase the risks of mercury poisoning by people using the still waters of the lake. What all of this means is that great care must be taken to maximise the benefits and minimise the costs if such schemes are to be established.

Fuelwood, charcoal and kerosene are the principal sources of household energy and are also used in industry and commerce. There are no reliable quantitative statistics available on biofuel usage but it is extensive. Much of this energy is not purchased as a commodity but rather it is collected for use in the home which can be extremely time consuming and arduous work, in particular for the women who may, in addition, have to collect drinking and washing water.[6]

The bauxite and sugar industries generate their own energy supply and the Guyana Electricity Corporation (GEC) generates the bulk of public supply. Electricity supply depends upon imported petroleum, with the exception of bagasse utilization in the sugar industry and the use of rice husks for electricity generation in a section of the rice industry. By the mid-1980s there was 385 mn kwh of generated electricity with 98.7% thermal production and 1.3% hydroelectric. The electricity sector faces a variety of financial, commercial, institutional and technical problems which together have resulted in a lack of supply reliability. There are investigations being undertaken concerning a possible Guyana-Venezuela grid link up based upon the importation of power from the huge Guri dam in Venezuela.

Sustainable development is all about making wise investments, conserving energy rather than building unrealistically high levels of capacity provision, which add to debt burdens and divert scarce investment resources into unproductive channels. There appears to be some scope for making greater use of indigenous renewable energy sources in the country.

Notes

1. E.I.U., *Guyana. Country Report*, 3rd Quarter, 1996, p.19.

2. *Guyana Review*, No 47, December 1996, p.5.

3. G. Sutton (1997), *op.cit*, December 1996, p.5.

4. D. Minott, "The potential of renewable energy in the Caribbean" in M.R. Bhagavan and S. Karekezi (eds), *Energy for Rural Development*, Zed Books, London, 1992, pp.211-218.

5. C. Caufield, *In the Rainforest*, Picador, London, 1986, p.17. The following two case studies on Surinam and Brazil are discussed in this book.

6. See Dankelman and Davidson (1988), *op.cit*, pp.83-85.

7 Biodiversity, tourism and the amerindian community

Biodiversity

Guyana does not possess the golden beaches of its Caribbean neighbours to attract the lucrative foreign exchange earning tourist trade. It does, however, possess a different kind of tourist asset, its forests and their incredible biodiversity. Guyana is the only English speaking country of the nine countries which form part of the Amazon basin. This obviously offers great eco-tourist potential for the North American market and thereby provides an important economic inducement to conserve forest areas, establish and manage national parks and integrate an eco-tourist component into other sectoral activities. Mining tracks can become wilderness trails. Porkknockers can earn money as tourist guides with panning for gold and diamonds as a component of foreign holiday tours. Management of forest reserves for tourist earning potential can become a component of private sector forest management.

Eco-tourist development means maintaining biodiversity. Maintaining biodiversity means conserving forests through the creation of national parks and reserves, by ensuring sustainable logging practices in the timber industry and by minimising the negative environmental effects of mining, road construction and settlement.

The positive economic value of good conservation practices is not confined by any means to the eco-tourist potential alone. The huge genetic resource base has enormous potential for making an important contribution to human progress across all sectors of activity, not least in medicine.[1] Wild species and varieties are used in the breeding of improved or specialised varieties of related crop species, in particular to increase yields and create resistance to pests and diseases. There is already an established trade in tropical wildlife that can be further developed but greater care is required to ensure long term sustainability. Over centuries the Amerindian community has lived in harmony with the forests and are a repository of wisdom concerning the sustainable utilisation of forest resources. The livelihood and cultural life of the Amerindian community is dependent upon conserving the forests and biodiversity. We will address the issue of the Amerindian community in greater detail subsequently

The difficulty of maintaining the rich biodiversity is a problem that Guyana shares with many countries in the South and this has been put succinctly by Deshmukh:

> Tropical countries are ecologically the best placed but economically poorly equipped to be in the forefront of genetic conservation. Much of the economic responsibility for this global concern clearly lies with the rich countries, many of which have irrevocably impoverished their own genetic resources. These countries should provide money and expertise to assist poor countries in the development of their own conservation programs. Such programs must reflect the aspirations and cultural background of the recipient countries rather than the priorities of the donor, if they are to be effective.[2]

A vast amount of work has still to be done to catalogue the biodiversity of Guyana. Some progress has been made however. In the early 1950s a preliminary survey of vegetation was undertaken.[3] Other work on the flora was published by Maguire[4] and Lindemann and Mori.[5] IUCN published a brief conservation survey in the late 1970s.[6] Of course there have been wider continental surveys of Latin America which provide much useful information.[7]

There is on-going work on the study of the country's rich biodiversity. Under the Amazon Cooperation Treaty there is collaboration with other national institutions including a botany project involving the University of Guyana (UG) and the Institute of Applied Science and Technology (IAST). Guyana also cooperates with the Commonwealth Science Council Biological Diversity and Genetic Resources Project. The Dept. of Biology at UG cooperates with the Flora of the Guianas Project which includes the Smithsonian Institute in Washington and the New York Botanical Gardens. Another initiative by the UK Open University in collaboration with GAHEF is the Guyana Rainforest Sustainability Programme. This initiative is the first on-the-ground work to take place within the area designated for the Programme for Sustainable Tropical Forestry. Twenty-two people began field work in the middle of 1992 to establish baseline data working in the Iwokrama area.[8] A local Biodiversity Society was established in 1991 which brought out its own newsletter *The Trumpeter*. As the first issue rightly pointed out: "Our knowledge of Guyana's biodiversity remains fragmentary and there is more than a lifetime's work to correct this".[9] Environmental issues did begin to register with radical political groups such as the WPA and Red Thread in the mid-1990s. Overall, however, environmental concerns are slow to take root in society.

Guyana is known to possess over 1,000 tree species and over 8,000 species of flora in the Highlands, with over half endemic species.[10] To date the following number of terrestrial vertebrate species are recorded: 728 bird species, 198 mammal species, 137 reptile species, and 105 amphibian species. In Table 2 a checklist is provided of wild fauna likely to be present within the 900,000 acre Programme for Sustainable Tropical Forestry (PSTF) reserve. The table also indicates: the approximate numbers of species, the listing of each species according to the Convention on International Trade in Endangered Species of Wild Fauna and Flora (CITES); the proposed listing of protected species within Guyana's Conservation of Wildlife Bill; and finally some indication of the potential economic importance.

The key to Guyana's immense potential wealth in its biodiversity lies in the maintenance of its forest resources. In neighbouring Brazil, Lutzenberger has done much to publicise the causes of the extensive deforestation occurring in that country.[11] This serves as a useful warning for Guyana not to make the same mistakes.

It is important to understand why the Amazonian forest is such a fragile system. We know from studies of the soils that they are poor in nutrients. This is confirmed by studies of Amazonian waters which are remarkable for their chemical purity and poor electrolytic content which makes them almost equivalent to rainwater. If the enormous vitality of the forest is not based upon highly fertile soils, on what does it depend? The answer lies in the closed circulation of nutrients between the multiple layers of biomass above the ground. The dense mat of tree roots near to the surface prevents the loss of the nutrients collected by the canopy and stem water run off. This is then recycled back into the living trees. The nutrients themselves come from the manure deposited by the fauna who live in and on the forest canopy and from the leaching effect of rainwater on the leaves and plants. The high degree of biodiversity facilitates the enormous number of sub-cycles of nutrient recycling which together create the whole complex system.

The World Bank in a 1991 report states unequivocally that "Unless forest management is invigorated, unscrupulous exploitation of the tropical forest could lead to serious environmental problems."[12] The report also concludes that in spite of conservation being the stated policy of government little has been done to intensify forest management and reforest logging areas. Maintaining diversity is essential for conservation and one of the best ways to ensure this is through the creation of national parks and reserves.

Tourism and national parks

There is currently only one legally protected park within the country - Kaieteur National Park, based around the spectacular falls on the Potaro River. In addition the NFAP proposes a further fifteen protected areas in addition to the expansion of Kaiteur.[13]

These are:

1. Biosphere reserve in the south west of Guyana.
2. Sea turtle sanctuary at Shell Beach.
3. Reserve in the Berbice Savannahs.
4. Protected area in the Kanuku Mountains.
5. Reserve at MMA for management of fish and game harvests.
6. Bird sanctuary at MMA on the Abary River.
7. MMA manatee sanctuary.
8. An international World Heritage Site in the Roraima area.
9. Protected area in the New River Triangle.
10. Wildlife sanctuaries on several Essequibo River islands.
11. Designate the longest free waterfall as a protected area.
12. Wildlife reserve within a section of the Dadanawa ranch area.
13. Protected area in the Yupukair-Annai North Savannah.
14. Protect part of the timber-commercial rainforest for study.
15. Develop the Mainstay Lakes area for domestic tourism.

This is project 22 within the STAP of the NFAP. The overall aim is to develop a network of protected areas to preserve the biological diversity found in Guyana and simultaneously to reduce the foreign debt whilst conserving its natural resources.

The NFAP project proposal summarizes well the situation:

A single protected area cannot ensure the long-term conservation of Guyana's biological diversity, nor the protection of its threatened and endangered species and natural ecosystems. Furthermore, despite its rich diversity of biological resources, no means are currently in place to tap the revenue earning potential of these resources through either tourism, fees for scientific study, or royalties other than from wildlife export, nor are there mechanisms to invite collaboration with international agencies interested in assisting in the establishment and management of protected areas in developing countries.[14]

The major constraints to the establishment of a system of protected areas in Guyana have been identified:[15]

- Lack of trained personnel at all levels (emigration of technical personnel);
- Lack of training facilities;
- Lack of policy concept, objectives and corresponding legislation;
- Overlapping legal authorities and management mandates;
- Insufficient inter-institutional planning and co-operation;
- Serious deterioration of the civil infrastructure over the past two decades;
- Adverse economic conditions with significant shortage of foreign exchange;
- Absence of environmental NGOs;
- Extremely low level of public awareness and interest;
- Lack of land use planning.

An important step forward on behalf of government commitment was the decision by the President of Guyana at the Commonwealth Heads of Government meeting in October 1989 to set aside 900,000 acres (360,000 ha) of Amazonian rain forest for a pilot protection scheme.

A proposal for realising a proper national park was advanced by GAHEF with the support of WWF for an expansion of Kaiteur to include the upper watershed of the Potaro River covering an area of 400,000 to 450,000 ha. No immediate decision was taken on the proposal.

Clarity over institutional responsibility for the national parks remained vague. The National Parks Commission Act gave responsibility for parks management to a voluntary body, the National Parks Commission. GAHEF, however, was charged with taking an active role in the establishment and management of protected areas. The Tourism Desk set up under the Ministry of Trade in 1987 claimed responsibility for all tourism related activities and GNRA with responsibility for mining and forestry exerted a powerful voice in this area of decision making. Coordination was weak between the Forestry Commission and the Geology and Mines Commission. This institutional confusion of mandates and conflicts over sectoral usage of the natural resource base has resulted in a failure to actively implement a national parks programme at Kaiteur or nationally.

Amerindian community

The relationship between the predominantly Afro Guyanese People's National Congress government which ruled Guyana from 1964 to 1992 and the

Amerindian community has been rather strained. There are historical reasons for this. The Dutch and then the British had used the Amerindians to hunt down escaped slaves and attack maroon settlements.[16] Rapid development of the economy and society along the coast in the 19th and 20th centuries led to the neglect of the forested interior and a disparaging of Amerindians by Afro and Indo Guyanese coastal communities. After independence the ruling party distrusted the Amerindians, according to Sanders, because they gave their electoral support to the United Force party and later the Guyana National Party, they were also accused of conspiring with Venezuela in its land claim to part of Guyana and there was an Amerindian insurrection in Rupununi in 1969.[17] Government took stern measures against suspected rebel leaders and kept tight security control subsequently.

Marcus Colchester has portrayed the situation over time almost as the swing of a pendulum from early days of Amerindian importance, a move away and now he argues a return of interest and importance once again.[18] When the Dutch first arrived in Guyana the base of the economy involved trade with the Amerindian communities of the interior, who furnished dyes, specialist woods, food and their labour in exchange for metal tools and other products. Then later the Amerindian community acted as a police force to keep the black slaves tied to the coast if any should try to escape. After the emancipation of the slaves from the 1840s onwards Amerindians became ever more marginalised. The economic focus moved to the coast and only now once again has it moved back to the interior with the massive increase in mining and timber exploitation when once again the Amerindians and their land rights have moved centre stage. At the heart of the matter is whose land is it? Land rights are at the centre of this complex problem and the issue is likely to be ongoing.

The situation of the Amerindians has been sympathetically and perceptively treated by Janette Forte.[19] She argues that the issue of Amerindian land rights was handled very tardily. The Amerindian Lands Commission made its recommendations in 1969. The government did not make its pronouncement on the issue until 1975, awarding only 1.39 million ha, less than a fifth of the land holding recommended by the commission, and considerably less than the land allocated to the Barama Company. Amerindians suffer disproportionately from poverty and disease and have been particularly badly hit by the economic restructuring programme as the costs of transport and services have massively increased. Forte puts forward a number of suggestions for improving the situation of the Amerindians including: not treating them as a security risk, encouraging more participation, settling land claims, involving them in ecotourism but not as exhibits, offering employment opportunities and education.

Marcus Colchester argues that the indigenous peoples and the rainforests are under threat as never before because an area the size of Portugal (almost nine million hectares) have been handed over to foreign logging companies, many with a less than perfect record, whilst a further area of territory, the size of the Netherlands, is under negotiation.[20] Further encroachments involve both mining concessions and the pressure from Brazil to complete the road link from its northern cities of Boa Vista and Manaus to a deep-sea container port near Georgetown.

Audrey Butt Colson has outlined many of the disruptive effects of the mining on the Amerindian communities.[21] Most of the mining as well as the timber concessions occur in the Amerindian areas of occupation in the interior. Up to 1996 around 3,000 prospecting licences have been granted and it is the Amerindian communities who bear the brunt of the impact of the mining. Traditionally the response of Amerindian communities has been to withdraw ever more into remote areas of the interior as outside incursions occur into their terrain.

What we are seeing now, I will argue, is a pincer movement which will limit ever more severely the room for manoeuvre of Amerindian communities. On the one hand, the government is granting more and more forest and mining concessions, encouraged by the structural adjustment programme. This is understandable in terms of promoting the country's development. Yet, serious questions remain about the safeguards meant to be in place to ensure sustainability and that the communities of the interior do not suffer as a result. These represent one arm of the pincer movement, coming from the coast. One the other hand there are incursions from the neighbouring states of the interior.

In the past, Amerindians retreating from incursions from the coast led on occasions to flirtations with neighbouring states in an effort to create room for manoeuvre.[22] Miners coming in from the neighbouring states are squeezing the Amerindian communities from the outside in. Indeed, the number of individual miners operating in the country is rapidly approaching the total Amerindian population.

Very little attention has been given to the effects of the massive increase in mining activities on the Amerindian communities. The remit of the state is very limited. The interior is characterised by a general lawlessness where power is determined by who exerts it on the ground. Both the small scale and the large scale mining operations have had a significant impact on the Amerindian communities.

The missile dredges have seriously impacted on the lives of local communities. The river is the community lifeline. The clear water, blackened by the tannin of the rainforest leaves, which is excellent to drink, bathe and wash clothes in, has been turned into a brown, sediment filled water course unfit for drinking, bathing, washing or for cooking water. Instead, people have to trek into the forest to find clean pockets of water and carry the water back to their homes. Fishing is also negatively affected, which traditionally provides a significant source of protein. Travel along the rivers becomes hazardous as a result of the disruptions and tailings piles of the missile dredges.

Health impacts of the mining are severe on Amerindian communities. As a result of the distortions created to the natural resource base typhoid, dysentery, malaria and mercury poisoning are being experienced. At a social level, sexually transmitted diseases are increasing including HIV/Aids infection. Traditionally under the prevailing sexual division of labour in the household, the men would provide the protein through hunting and fishing, they would clear the land for cultivation and so on. With the introduction of mining the old ways fall apart. Men no longer marry, then go to live with their in-laws and support them as in the past. There is an atomisation and break-up of traditional communities. Men earn far more cash from mining, alcoholism and other vices enter the community. Collective social norms are replaced by a growing individualism. Where before there was collective self-reliance on their own community this is being replaced by ever more reliance on outside forces, notably mining interests which are not under the control of Amerindian communities themselves. For the critics, this represents a great danger.[23] The men are no longer around to instruct the next generation of males about the ways of the past. The rich source of traditional knowledge is being lost. Indeed, Conrad Gorinsky argues there is an immense problem with the loss of the enormously rich traditional body of knowledge.[24]

At the centre of debate, all agree, lies the land issue. Whilst only being a small minority of the total population the Amerindian community has a special importance as the traditional land use managers of the forest interior. As a result of holding a crucial electoral political balance of power through the United Front party in the early 1960s, the Amerindian community was fortunate to win the promise of some land rights. In this regard they were more able than some Amerindian communities in neighbouring countries. Even so, and slowed down by the Rupununi rebellion in 1969, it was not until 1976 that a legislative act was passed giving land titles. Yet critics, such as Colchester, point out that Amerindians who are a majority in the interior have title to only 800,000 hectares, whilst 9,000,000 hectares have been handed out as timber concessions.[25]

Furthermore, the legal base for the Amerindian land titles remains unresolved and no Amerindian land claims have ever gone to court.[26] The PPP Civic party when it stood in the 1992 election promised to give proper land rights to the Amerindian community. This did not happen. Yet there are signs of more articulated voices emerging for Amerindian rights with the more democratic political dispensation of the 1990s. The first such organisation was the Amerindian Peoples Association (APA) set up in 1991. For better or worse, a number of other organisations have also been established including the Amerindian Action Movement of Guyana, the Guyana Organisation of Indigenous Peoples and yet another self-designated national Amerindian organisation. There is a fragmentation of the Amerindians' voice within civil society and this is encouraged both by local self-interest and by outside players.

So in conclusion, what are the prospects? Whoever controls the government in the current era will rely upon the mineral and forest resources of the interior as the greatest revenue generating opportunity. The fragmented voice of the Amerindian communities, supported by international organisations such as the World Rainforest Movement and its Forest Peoples Programme can exert a moderating influence via the key aid donors, as was the case in relation to the UK's ODA agreement with the Government of Guyana to freeze further logging concessions, as agreed for a three year period in 1994. It seems unlikely that the political leverage of the Amerindian community will prove sufficient to realise its new claim to hold ownership of the underground mineral resources. Quite simply there is too much at stake.

The onus remains on the international community in particular to decide if it really wants to maintain the existing tropical rainforest with all of the potential benefits for stabilising global environmental change and maintaining invaluable biodiversity. If it does wish to preserve a rather unique and intact pocket of tropical rainforest, then it has to be prepared to pay for it. If not, then the international community must be prepared to carry the long term costs. For one of the poorest countries in the Western hemisphere, it is unrealistic to expect any government to constrain avenues for economic development. Under existing structural adjustment programmes the capacity of the state to exercise effective controls appears to be limited given tight restrictions on government expenditure. If the international community shows willing to fund it and the government demonstrates its determination to enforce it, then the Amazonian rainforest can be preserved.

Notes

1. See for example, M.J. Balick, "Useful plants of the Amazon" in G. Prance and T. Lovejoy (eds), *Key Environments: Amazonia*, Pergamon Press, Oxford, 1985.

2. I. Deshmuckh, *Ecology and Tropical Biology*, Blackwell Scientific Publications, Oxford, 1986, p.321.

3.   D.B. Fanshaw, *The vegetation of British Guyana: a preliminary review*, Institute Paper No 29, Imperial Forest Institute, Oxford, 1952.

4.   B. Maguire, "On the flora of the Guyana Highfield", *Biogropica*, Vol 2 No 2, 1970, pp.85-100.

5.   J.C. Lindemann and S.A. Mori, "The Guiannas" in D. Campbell and D. Dammond (eds), *Floristic Inventory of Tropical Countries*, New York Botanical Garden, New York, 1989.

6.   A. Dalfelt, *Nature conservation survey of the Republic of Guyana*, IUCN, mimeo, 1978.

7.   See for example, J. Dorst, *South America and Central America - a Natural History*, Random House, New York, 1967.

8.   Personal communication with Mike Gillman, Open University, UK, 13 October 1992.

9.   Robert Brown, in *The Trumpeter*, Vol 1 No 1, 1991, p.10.

10.   B. Maguire (1970), *op.cit.*

11.   See for example, Jose Lutzenberger "Who is destroying the Amazon Rainforest", *The Ecologist*, Vol 17, No 4/5, 1987, pp.155-160.

12.   World Bank (1991), *op.cit*, p.16.

13.   *NFAP, op.cit.*

14.   *ibid*, pp.35-36.

15.   G. Schuerholz, *Kaiteur National Park, Guyana, Diagnostic Report*, GAHEF, Ministry of Trade and WWF, March 1991.

16.   C. Henfrey, *The Gentle People*, Hutchinson, London 1964, p.263.

17.   A. Sanders, *The Powerless People*, Macmillan, London, 1987.

18. M. Colchester, *Guyana: fragile frontier: miners, loggers and forest peoples*, Latin America Bureau, London, 1997[1].

19. J. Forte, *"Amerindians and Poverty"*, a paper prepared by the Amerindian Research Unit for the Institute of Development Studies seminar on Poverty, 19 March 1993.

20. M. Colchester, "Guyana: fragile frontier", *Race and Class*, Vol 38, No 4, 1997(b), pp.33-56.

21. A.B. Coulson, *"Impact of mining developments on Amerindian communities in Interior Guyana,"* a paper given at the conference on Environment and Development in Guyana, Centre for Developing Areas Research, Royal Holloway, University of London, 7 May 1997.

8 Towards a national strategy for sustainability

It is essential to adopt an anticipatory, cross-sectoral approach to decision making if development is to take place in a more sustainable manner. This is so important because following the democratic elections of October 1992 and the renewed economic impetus within the country there has been a considerable increase in economic activity. Yet this is notoriously difficult to achieve. This chapter indicates how some of the foundations could be laid for just such an integrated approach. The passage on coastal zone management serves to highlight the need for this in practical terms.

Rio earth summit and its legacy

The major sustainable development international initiative of the 1990s has been the United Nations Conference on Environment and Development (UNCED) held in 1992. What contribution if any, could the Earth Summit held in the neighbouring country of Brazil, make to Guyana's policy development process?

Firstly, and very positively, Guyana participated fully in the global environmental summit held over the border and acted as a spokesperson on behalf of the Caribbean community. As an active member of the UNCED process, Guyana offered a commitment to build upon the achievements of this historic summit. The major outputs from the conference and their implications for Guyana are outlined below.

The Rio Framework Convention on Climate Change emerged following the threat of rapid climate change and rising sea levels as a result of emissions of greenhouse gases. Given Guyana's population concentration along the low lying coastal strip and the high level of vulnerability of its economy and peoples to possible rises in the sea level, this treaty is very important for Guyana's long term future. Guyana's interests lie in helping to ensure compliance with the treaty. Nations ratifying the treaty have to submit reports setting out what they are doing to ascertain emission levels. Basically this is aimed at the developed nations, who caused the problem in the first place, and they were requested to

73

stabilise their emissions at 1990 levels by the year 2000. At a follow-up meeting, five years on from the Rio summit, held in mid-1997, it was apparent that very few of the industrialised countries had made significant progress in this regard and the United States was singled out for its negligence. The treaty was not binding in this regard but merely encouraged countries to adopt measures to reduce emissions. It also encouraged the transfer of environmentally sound technologies and know-how from the developed countries, a key demand by the South and one that is important for Guyana given the current expansion of mining, forestry, industry and other sectoral activities. The US government endeavoured to placate its critics at the 1997 meeting by making a commitment to help developing nations reduce their emission levels.

The Convention on Biological Diversity is a declaration of intent rather than a binding agreement to conserve the diversity of plant and animal species within national borders. There is provision for support from the developed to the developing countries to help realise this goal. Guyana is well placed to take advantage of this commitment in shaping its development strategy, given the richness of its biodiversity.

Whilst both conventions were rather watered down at Rio, mainly as a result of US opposition, it is possible that these will be given more muscle in the future. That was the case with the Vienna Convention on the ozone layer of 1985 which, with the signing of the Montreal protocol two years later, became more of a force to reckon with. Undeniably, this will require a more serious level of political commitment throughout the international community to ensure effective action. This will remain as a challenge well into the 21st century.

The text on Forest Principles whilst being non-binding, lays down important principles for forest management. Although the North wanted a binding forest convention, the Group of 77, the countries of the South, refused, on the grounds that unless the North provided funds to compensate for the preservation of the forests then they would have to use the forest for development purposes as it formed part of their natural resource endowment. The North wanted conservation of the tropical forests to act as a carbon sink whilst being unwilling to tackle seriously carbon dioxide emissions in their own countries, in the eyes of the critics. These tensions continue to be unresolved as we enter the new millennium. They will not readily go away.

The Rio Declaration on Environment and Development provides a series of commonly agreed principles to help member states adopt national policies which encourage a more sustainable development future. Of the 27 principles for protecting the environment included in the declaration, it is significant that the emphasis is on maximising popular participation. Principle 10 states:

Environmental issues are best handled with the participation of all concerned citizens ... States shall facilitate and encourage public awareness and participation by making information widely available.

The organisation of a national conference on environment and development soon after the People's Progressive Party/Civic Coalition came to power in October 1992 under President Jagan demonstrated a positive commitment by the new government to encourage greater participation.

Principle 22 notes that:

Indigenous people and their communities, and other local communities, have a vital role in environmental management and development because of their knowledge and traditional practices. States should recognise and duly support their identity, culture and interests and enable their effective participation in the achievement of sustainable development.

Politically, in the midst of a global recession it was obviously difficult to get governments to think too much in the long term rather than short term. But Principle 3 of the Rio Declaration states clearly that in meeting today's needs, nations should not so degrade the environment and squander their natural resources such that future generations are compromised in meeting their own needs. This is close to a full endorsement of the Brundtland definition of sustainable development which marked such an important step forward in global thinking with the publication in 1987 of "Our Common Future". Finally, mention must be made of the importance given by the Rio Declaration to states enacting effective environmental legislation (Principle 11). It is vital that recommendations are made on legislative policy for the structure, functions, content and scope of intersectoral and sectoral environmental legislation and the power and duties of related institutions as well as their relations between themselves.

Agenda 21 is a massive and comprehensive document covering all areas of activity necessary to ensure a more sustainable development future. The long term post-Rio challenge involves moving ahead with national strategies for sustainability, thereby making Agenda 21 operational.

We will now turn to address some of the specific intersectoral challenges for sustainable development, beginning with coastal zone management.

Coastal zone management

Marine and coastal areas are the ultimate recipients of the effects of environmental degradation and pollution released in the air, on land and in the water. The coastal zone is at the epicentre of potential sectoral conflicts over natural resource use. It is here, for example, that the effects of mercury pollution and alterations in the river flow caused by gold and diamond mining inland have their effects upon the fisheries sector and public health.

Coastal ecosystems in the tropics possess the most productive and ecologically diverse systems on Earth. As Carleton Ray has noted:

> Unfortunately, the threats that humankind pose to coastal and marine ecosystems are often obscure and related to the still poorly understood processes that drive ecosystems.[1]

Environmental problems and natural resource deterioration are quite literally obscured by being under the water's surface. No longer can the situation of "out of sight, out of mind" prevail, as the quality of the water resource no less than the quality of the soil is vital for continued human existence and development.

There are a number of threats to the coastal zone ecosystem which may impede future development potential. The first concerns soil erosion both at the coast and along the banks of rivers that converge on the coast. The latter results from alluvial mining and logging in the interior along with human settlements and agricultural production in the coastal zone itself. Siltation of coastal and riverine waters can seriously decrease their productivity and threaten domestically produced protein intake from the artesanal fisheries sector and industrial sector export earnings as the fish and shrimp nursery is gradually destroyed. Clearing of coastal vegetation, in particular the mangrove forests, may have very serious effects upon coastal zone protection, the vitality of the fisheries sector and the maintenance of high biodiversity which is so important given that Guyana's future tourist potential lies predominantly through eco-tourism. The rebuilding of the coastal protection system, the revitalisation of the drainage and irrigation systems, the expansion of agricultural activities with an increasing use of agrochemicals, the ever growing population and settlement concentration on the coast, altogether place enormous pressures on existing coastal vegetation. Destruction of the mangroves increases coastal erosion and sedimentation with all of the attendant effects outlined above. Quarrying will have to expand in the north west of the country to rebuild the sea defences.

Overfishing is clearly a serious problem. It raises important issues in the medium term concerning domestic versus foreign exploitation of the resource base, food production versus export earnings. There is also the problem of illegal encroachment within the 200 mile sovereignty limit and the capacity of the government to monitor and control this. Given the complexity of the intersectoral use of the resource base it is clearly imperative to develop an integrated and sustainable strategy for coastal zone management.

Meeting the sustainable development challenge

Instituting effective natural resource management requires reasonably reliable resource inventories. To complement the information on resource availability reliable information is also needed on resource use. Reliable data on resource availability and use is not presently available in mining, forestry, agriculture, fishing, human settlement and service provision. It is particularly weak concerning overall biodiversity. It is one thing to have the data. It is quite another to build a consensus on the right balance of resource use with those whose livelihoods depend upon utilising a particular resource. All too frequently, we have the problem known as the tragedy of the commons. Each user of the common resource has much to gain individually by increasing his or her exploitation of the resource even if this produces diminishing returns overall. Hence short term gain and self interest leads the individual to maximise his or her own use of the common resource to everyone's, including their own, long term detriment. For this reason the state has an important role to play to ensure that the long term interests of everyone are safeguarded.

The challenge of ensuring long term development which is properly sustainable certainly requires an enlightened and informed approach by government. But this alone is not sufficient. Governments and state structures in developing countries experiencing economic crisis, debt and a heavy burden of past policy shortcomings have a limited capacity to respond to the challenge of sustainability. Indeed, the very idea of the government alone ensuring sustainability is against the core principle of sustainable development which is all about people taking responsibility themselves. The government's role should be that of facilitator. Governments alone do not have the necessary resources, be they human, material or financial. Indeed the role of government is anyway constrained within an international climate which encourages an increasing move to market rather than state initiatives.

This is not to deny a vital role for the state, especially in fact, because of an increasing reliance on market and private enterprise initiatives. This is precisely because whilst private enterprise may help the growth dynamic, it tends to be enterprise specific in its goals of profit maximisation and sectoral specific in its orientation (enterprises in gold mining may find reason to make common cause together in certain instances). It is difficult under a private enterprise economy to move beyond profit maximisation and sectoral interests to achieve a more rational and sustainable utilisation nationally of the resource base. But there are certainly ways of encouraging this, not least by opening up the debate and allowing enlightened self-interest to enter in. In other words, if sectoral interests are collectively aware of the intersectoral issues that affect them, and possibilities of conflicts over resource use then they can act with the government to try to find a solution. A strengthened civil society will ensure that these issues encourage public debate and accountability.

In many cases improved resource management principles can be introduced in the sectors to ensure both higher profits and more benign environmental effects. The process of state divestiture of enterprises should seek to maximise such developments. Where this involves negotiating concessions for resource use over time then it may be well to consider whether longer term time horizons for concessions may encourage more sustainable practices. Secondly, if multi-sectoral resource use is negotiated then the enterprise will be confronted directly with the issue of sustainability.

Considerable work is going on in the field of environmental economics trying to show how managing the economy in a different manner can minimise negative environmental impacts. If we take the case of deforestation in Amazonia, in neighbouring Brazil, the evidence presented by David Pearce suggests that economic incentives have been instrumental in the deforestation including road-building programmes, subsidised credit for crop and livestock development, lack of security of tenure for forest dwellers and market forces operating within the current constraints of a distorted valuation of tropical forests.[2] He proposes an approach known as Total Economic Value (TEV), which is a different concept from financial value. Hence the TEV in the context of tropical forests would include:

Direct Value:	Sustainable timber, non-timber products, recreation, medicine, plant genetics, education, human habitat.
Indirect Value:	Nutrient cycling, watershed protection, air pollution reduction, microclimatic functions, carbon store.
Option Value:	Future uses of the direct and indirect value (see below).
Existence Value:	Forest as object of intrinsic value, as a bequest, stewardship responsibility including cultural heritage values, biodiversity.

Direct-use values include timber and non-timber products and eco-tourism. Indirect-use values refer to the ecological functions of tropical forests - mineral cycling and watershed protection. Existence value is unrelated to use but resides in the value of the forest in itself. Pearce concludes that there is some evidence that direct-use values alone favour forest conservation. Hence in Brazil, take-away the subsidies and forest clearance for livestock production has no financial rationale.

The key problem for poor developing countries is how to appropriate in practice the non-cash elements of the TEV. Pearce writes:

> Since much of the option and existence value associated with tropical forests accrues to people outside of the tropically forested countries, appropriation involves cash or other resource transfers from rich to poor countries.[3]

Clearly this is something that the Government of Guyana has to fight for in collaboration with other countries in a similar situation, Yet there are several precedents. The Montreal Protocol transfers cash to developing countries to compensate for their foregoing of CFCs use. Debt-for-nature swaps offer another example. Finally the Global Environmental Facility is intended to take such matters into account.

Michael Richards, in a recent study of rapid land turnover in colonisation zones of Amazonia, indicates the importance of institutional factors and market incentives rather than land productivity in determining colonist farmer stability. As farming in the forest frontier matures, farmer responses to economic and institution factors change, this is the "moving target" in the title of Richards' work. His study reinforces our central argument that more integrated policy, institutional and technical strategies are essential for success.[4] This is important whether new valuations of tropical forests are adopted as Pearce proposes or farming colonisation occurs.

At a more intangible level but non the less important is the international perception of how seriously a government is taking issues of environmental conservation in the context of attempting to devise a sustainable development national strategy. Hence positive perceptions of governmental efforts in Costa Rica have served to attract considerable international financing. It is far from certain that all the solutions to a more sustainable development future lie in efforts by Pearce and his collaborators in the London Environmental Economics Centre who strive to put a monetary value on every aspect of the environment. Their efforts surely have a role to play. Yet perhaps paradoxically, taking the moral high ground and being perceived to be taking a positive moral stand for environmental conservation could be an effective way of attracting international financial support. Integrity is the most valuable commodity of all. Looking back on Guyana's recent past, there was clearly a problem in attracting international support both for the National Forestry Action Programme and the Programme for Sustainable Tropical Forestry. The latter is now within Global Environmental Facility funding but there has been considerably delay in getting anything going on the ground.

Guyana has a growing body of literature on which to build to help devise an effective national strategy for sustainable development. Two key early documents are a report by Christopher Pastakia in 1989[5] and Guyana's national report to the UNCED conference of 1992.[6] An important step forward was made when a short Environmental Policy document was approved by Cabinet in December 1990 which committed the government to adopting and implementing a national policy for environmental management and sustainable development. The policy set out the following basic principles.

In order to conserve and improve the environment, the Government of Guyana will endeavour:

-    to assure all people living in the country the fundamental right to an environment, adequate for their health and well-being.
-    to achieve a balance between the use and conservation of the nation's resources to meet the needs of economic development and improved standards of living.
-    to ensure that, where environmental damage occurs, remedial action will be taken either by the agency or individual responsible for such damage, failing which by GAHEF or an independent designated agency, with the cost being recovered from the agency or individual causing the environmental damage.
-    premised on the principle of the exercise of sovereignty, to conserve and use the environment and national resources of Guyana for the benefit of both present and future generations.
-    to maintain ecosystems and ecological processes essential for the functioning of the biosphere; to preserve biological diversity, and to observe the principle of optimum sustainable yield in the use of renewable natural resources and ecosystems both on land and the sea.
-    to rehabilitate damaged ecosystems where possible and reverse any degradation of the environment.
-    to ensure prior environmental assessments of proposed activities which may significantly affect the environment.
-    ensure that conservation is treated as an integral part of the planning and implementation of development activities.

-    to promote the pursuance of international co-operation on environmental issues.
-    to raise the level of consciousness of the population on the environmental implications of economic and social activities through comprehensive education and public awareness programmes.
-    to involve the population in the management of the environment and resources.

The strategy devised to implement this policy involved defining both a legal and institutional framework. A draft National Environment Protection Act was formulated but never passed by the Hoyte government. A high priority was to place a National Environmental Protection Act onto the statute books. Some early progress was made in establishing a high level institutional forum for intersectoral co-operation, when in September 1991 Cabinet agreed to the formation of an Interagency Committee on the Environment, represented at ministerial and permanent secretary level, chaired by GAHEF as the lead agency responsible for the environment. The new government will keep under review the process of reorganising the institutional framework. An early move which was potentially encouraging, with the new Jagan government, was the formation of an Environment Division within the Office of the President. This was followed by the creation of an Environment Protection Agency, given considerably greater powers in relation to land policy, which offered the prospect at least, of greater coordination, although the threat would remain of a new agency merely establishing duplicate structures for oversight of mining, forests and other natural resource exploitation. Undeniably there was a centralising of power in relation to the environment and natural resource use with the growing power of EPA and a more direct involvement of the Presidency in the late 1990s. The new government has to develop its policy framework and also help establish the legal and institutional framework to put this policy into practice. A Natural Resources Advisory Board is in operation involving many of the institutional stakeholders. A draft national environment action plan was first prepared by the Hoyte government. However this tended to emphasise technical aspects of monitoring and control rather than education and improved sectoral coordination. The latter represents a more proactive approach whilst the former is more defensive. An active approach will demonstrate the positive advantages that can accrue by improved integration of environment and development concerns and is the preferable alternative.

Further policy developments in the late 1990s included a National Biodiversity Plan, financed by the UNDP. The plan was completed in 1997 and was then submitted for Cabinet consideration. A National Biodiversity Committee was also established. The Carter Centre in Georgetown supported the formulation of a land-use policy guidance document. Many more initiatives of this nature need to be encouraged to build a more integrated and effective approach to natural resource usage.

Yet there remains a worrying policy inertia. The National Forestry Action Programme remained dormant, lacking any funding or staff. The National Environment Action Programme will only move forward when a legislative and institutional format is finally put in place. For critics, there were signs that things were moving in the wrong direction as the three year moratorium on granting further forestry concessions appeared to be eroding in 1997, and fears were expressed that the interior was being sold off wholesale to foreign mining and logging companies at the expense primarily of the Amerindian peoples.[7]

Global Initiatives

Since the Stockholm Environment Conference held in 1972, which alerted the World to the issues, the international community has progressed significantly in moving towards agreement on a number of guiding principles to help nations shape their national strategies for integrating environment and development concerns. This approach has become widely known as sustainable development. Most nations have now declared their commitment to find sustainable development policy solutions. A growing literature exists on this subject and a growing number of commitments by the nations of the world have been made, to work both collectively to find solutions to the developmental and environmental problems of the planet, and individually at the national level, to ensure that the commitments on paper are put into policy practice.

Towards the end of 1991 the World Conservation Union (IUCN), the United Nations Environment Programme (UNEP) and the World Wide Fund for Nature (WWF) published *Caring for the World. A Strategy for Sustainability*. This document moved far beyond the earlier World Conservation Strategy of 1980 in its efforts to integrate the economic, social and ecological requirements for sustainability. The three main obstacles to sustainability outlined in this report are the lack of an ethical commitment, an inequitable distribution of power and the persistent notion that conservation and development can be managed separately.

Eight key principles for sustainability emerge:

1.   Limit human impact on the biosphere to a level within carrying capacity.
2.   Maintain the stock of biological wealth.
3.   Use non renewable resources at rates not exceeding the creation of renewable substitutes.

4.   Aim for an equitable distribution of the benefits and costs of resource use and environmental management.
5.   Promote technologies that increase the benefits from a given stock of resources.
6.   Use economic policy to help maintain natural wealth.
7.   Adopt an anticipatory, cross-sectoral approach to decision making.
8.   Promote and support cultural values compatible with sustainability.

At the crucial policy and institutional level, principle seven is particularly important. The document spells out the three main requirements here:

-    Long term not short term planning horizons.
-    Greater anticipation and prevention rather than reaction and cure.
-    Provide agencies responsible for sectors that share resources and environments with shared objectives and policies that oblige them to work together.

There are three systems basic to any process of development: the biological or ecological resource system, the economic system, and the social system. Human society applies a set of goals to each system. For example, in the ecological system to protect biodiversity, in the economic system to increase production of goods and services, and in the social system to ensure broad public participation in decision making.

The objective of sustainable development is to maximise goal achievement across the three systems at one and the same time through an adaptive process of trade-offs. It is adaptive because individual preferences, social norms, ecological conditions, and the state of development change over time. Agenda 21 of the UNCED Conference repeatedly emphasises these three systems and the need to apply an integrated approach to them.

Chapter 8 of Agenda 21 outlines the key objectives in helping to formulate a national strategy for sustainable development.

These objectives include:

-    Integration of environment and development at all levels in decision making, thereby strengthening institutional structures.
-    A long term, coherent and cross-sectoral approach, which takes into account the linkages between the various political, economic, social and environmental issues.

- Systematic and ongoing review, monitoring and evaluation of the development process and the environment.
- Participatory development and social partnership, improving mechanisms for a broader involvement in decision-making at every level thereby mobilising a wider range of actors and ensuring their commitment and a more equitable definition of needs.
- Greater accountability, transparency in decision-making and access to information.
- Setting clear, achievable, costed and time-bound targets, goals and objectives.
- Defining ecological and other constraints on human and economic activity.
- Rationalising and integrating existing national planning exercises, and where relevant subsume donor action plans into a country-driven process.
- Creating a framework for implementing Agenda 21.
- Creating a framework for accountability and transparency on environment and development issues.
- Examining the interface between national development and environment, and international factors.

Added to these are the following general objectives:

* *Setting targets and goals*
  Setting clear goals and objectives for each sector of society, and being accountable for meeting them.
* *Trade-offs*
  A statement indicating the trade-offs and priorities between the economic, social, and ecological systems making the compromises clear and transparent, and ensuring that differing viewpoints are represented and where possible resolved.
* *Constraints*
  Anticipating and defining the ecological and other constraints within which human and economic activity must abide if development is to be sustainable. This makes the future less surprising, minimizing risks and enhancing the capacity to cope. It is better to know the limitations sooner rather than later.
* *Rationalising existing initiatives*
  There is an obvious need to coordinate and rationalise existing national planning exercises, whether these are national, sectoral plans, NGO plans, or the many donor action plans.

*   *Framework for implementing Agenda 21*
    Practical implementation of Agenda 21 will require that it is both disaggregated and built-up in the national context. This hugely complex task will be made easier if it fits into a well coordinate national strategy.
*   *International/National constraints/opportunities*
    The national sustainable development strategy can provide the opportunity to rigorously examine how international factors affect national environment and development concerns, and clearly trade, debt, and international economic issues will be uppermost concerns. These will also be relevant to developed countries, but greater emphasis will need to be placed on the degree to which a nation's resource consumption affects the environment of other countries.
    Each government is called upon to adopt a national strategy for sustainable development, to build a national consensus and formulate capacity-building strategies for implementing Agenda 21.

Capacity-building is a major dimension of implementation and covers technology transfer, science for sustainable development, education, public awareness and training and national strategies for sustainability. Capacity-building is undoubtedly seen as a major area for future international cooperation. A Sustainable Development Commission was established at Rio to oversee progress towards implementation of Agenda 21 and reporting through the Economic and Social Council to the UN General Assembly.

There is clearly much still to do in building a national strategy for sustainability which takes and adapts lessons from global initiatives and endeavours to apply them creatively to the specific circumstances in Guyana.

Notes

1. G. Carleton Ray, "Sustainable use of the Global Ocean" in D.B. Botkin, M.F. Caswell, J.E. Estate and A.A. Orio (eds), *Changing the Global Environment: Perspectives on Human Involvement*, Academic Press, Boston, 1989, p.84.

2. David Pearce, "Deforesting the Amazon: Toward an Economic Solution" *Ecodecision* (Canada) Vol 1 No 1, 1991, pp.40-48. See also David Pearce "An Economic Approach to Saving the Tropical Forests" in Dieter Helm (ed), *Economic Policy Towards the Environment*, Blackwell, Oxford, 1991 and David Pearce (ed), *Blueprint 2*, Earthscan, London, 1991, Chapter 8.

3. *ibid*, (Pearce in *Ecodecision*), p.48.

4. M. Richards, *Missing a Moving Target? Colonist Technology Development on the Amazon Frontier*, ODI, London, 1997.

5. Christopher Pastakia, *Assessment of Institutional Capabilities in Environmental Management and Proposals for Institutional Strengthening*, a report for GAHEF under Inter-American Development Bank Technical Co-operation, December 1989.

6. GAHEF (1991), *op.cit.*

7. M. Colchester, *Guyana. Fragile Frontier*, Latin America Bureau, London, 1997.

9 The institutional challenge

Institutional structures

Strengthening institutions and improving institutional coordination are essential for sustainable development. We will analyse in detail the recent history of Guyana's institutional structures, their respective areas of activity and where the major institutional challenges lie. It is all too easy to lose valuable institutional memory. The past has many lessons for the future. The change of government naturally invoked a desire to create new structures. Such an exercise works best when the lessons of the past have been well imbibed. In Guyana as in many other developing countries, the institutional structures grew up piecemeal and frequently there is a lack of clarity over mandates and an even more worrying incapacity to facilitate successful institutional coordination to ensure that both development and environment concerns are given proper consideration. Above all it is important to draw out carefully the lessons of the past, in relation to the strengths and weaknesses of institutional formations.

The problems facing all of the institutional structures have been a reflection of the sorry state of the economy. The heavy burden of debt and structural adjustment makes it hard to ensure the necessary strengthening of state institutions. The move towards divestiture of state assets creates a more vibrant private sector able to attract talented individuals away from public service. It was no more easy before the readjustments, as the economic decline precipitated on enormous exodus of skilled people abroad. Moreover the decline in the economy inevitably meant that the country's educational system experienced a similar demise. All institutions are now struggling to provide the pay and conditions to attract staff and the transport, equipment and resources in general to make their presence effective. There has been a massive brain drain from the country and whilst highly qualified Guyanese are helping say, to keep the health services going in the United Kingdom, Canada and the United States, the health service in Guyana has been deteriorating. The country has an abundance of highly skilled and talented people, the problem is that their skills are being employed in other countries rather than in their own. Some benefits do accrue to the country, but mainly as financial remittances to remaining family members.

We will look at the main institutions in turn.

The environment

It is important to review the evolution of the institutional structures dealing with the environment as this is a relatively new area of government concern and there have been significant changes in recent years. The Guyana Agency for Health Sciences, Education, Environment and Food Policy (GAHEF) was established under the Public Corporation Act of 1988. It was formerly the Ministry of Medical Education, Environment and Food Policy. The move from being a ministry to becoming a parastatal was made precisely in an effort to create more attractive conditions to employ and maintain staff. Whereas specific salary levels were laid down for the civil service, there was far greater flexibility for the parastatals. Only with the formation of GAHEF did the environment begin to figure in a serious way within the institutional structures of government. GAHEF had five different divisions:

i)   Health Sciences Education Division;
ii)   Environment Division;
iii)   Food and Nutrition Division;
iv)   Veterinary Public Health Unit;
v)   Food and Drugs Division.

According to the National Environmental Strategy at the time, GAHEF was charged with: providing monitoring and control services; promoting research and studies; providing guidance on environmental matters; maintaining a databank; training of staff; public education and coordinating environmental activities.

The Environment was the youngest division in GAHEF hence faced a considerable challenge in developing its activities and training the skilled staff able to ensure successful implementation.[1] Whilst GAHEF had a very dynamic executive director there was no qualified middle management to head the environment division. Indeed, there was no one with even a Masters degree in the division. The country as a whole lacked people qualified in environmental issues. The professional staff were all young, had a first degree from the University of Guyana and no specialised training, although a few had done some short courses. An Environment Research and Information Unit used to be based at the Institute of Applied Science and Technology (IAST) located on the University campus until it was dissolved in 1989 and GAHEF took over the mandate. Only the Senior Environment Officer remained from the original IAST staff.

With young staff possessing no specialist training, without a head of division and with few resources, not surprisingly the new division was unable to adequately fulfil the tasks to which it has been assigned in the early 1990s. Without exception, all members of staff needed specialised training in their designated areas of responsibility. Key problems in institutional capacity building aside from human resource development, included the absence of a clear legislative mandate for the operations of the division and a lack of clarity over institutional areas of responsibility. Each member of staff had a prime responsibility for one main area of activity but also made an all round contribution to the work of the division. Key areas of activity included: pollution, environment education, mining, coastal zone management and forestry.

Work related to pollution involved the investigation of nuisance complaints against cottage industries, in particular bad smells and noise pollution. A major complaint concerned the effects of crop spraying of rice on the surrounding populations. In this case a joint investigative mission was launched by both the Environment and Food and Drugs Divisions in 1992 in which the author was able to participate directly.

Environmental education activities began in a structured way in 1990. Before there were only ad hoc schools' talks. In the following two years seven seminars were held in six administrative regions of the country. Six of these two day seminars had school teachers as the target. The objectives of these seminars were to: create and develop an awareness of the environment amongst teachers; educate teachers in basic environmental concepts and in the important environmental issues facing Guyana.

The format was generally a first day of lectures and videos and in the second day group discussion related to the specific environmental problems of the region and how teachers could help deal with these problems. In addition, two or three of the teachers attending would be asked to give a presentation adapting the materials they had received to the needs of the particular age group that they were teaching. Visual aids were displayed, including those connected with health education, demonstrating intra-GAHEF divisional coordination.

A schools competition was regularly held for essays and poster design, both at the regional and national level, with an award ceremony held on Environment Day. Concerning health education, awards were given for the best kept school and the most improved school. The Canadian International Development Agency (CIDA) provided some material support for these initiatives. A pamphlet was produced called *Man and the Environment* with 5000 duplicated copies printed.

A major bottleneck for the programme was the high cost of travel to the regions. Chartering a plane cost G.$140,000, at early 1990s exchange rates, a huge sum for an Environment division with limited resources. In order to maximise the benefits, in addition to the two day seminar, the division did a further two days of school talks in the regions visited.

Other initiatives included a television programme produced at a cost of G.$50,000. Also daily radio broadcasts were initiated for a year, running five days per week, at a cost of only US $3,000. This also acted as an important incentive to the professional staff who enjoyed writing and presenting the material and the personal cudos it entailed being media presenters. The exercise itself was very educational as it required of the staff analytical work to grasp the essentials of their task and the ability to transform this into a readily understandable message.

Education and public awareness initiatives beginning in this modest manner are precisely what has to be built upon for the future. This is an essential priority. These experiences are positive examples of effective activity that need to be developed and expanded.

Severe problems are involved in monitoring the extensive and serious environmental impacts of mining activities. Firstly there are the logistical and financial difficulties of travelling to monitor the effects of mining operations deep in the interior. Reaching these requires either a very expensive aeroplane charter or spending weeks in overland travel. If samples are taken to measure the possible effects of using mercury in gold mining, the next problem is how to get the samples analysed. There used to be such a capacity within the IAST but their instruments had ceased to be functional. A further complication is involved if there are long delays in getting samples to a laboratory abroad. This is particularly the case with the cold vapour testing technique. An additional difficulty is the human resource scarcity, as there are not the people available to spend long periods of time in the interior monitoring the environmental effects of various mining activities.

All of these inadequacies came into the spotlight with the Omai gold mine environmental disaster in 1995. The point is, such weaknesses were evident from the early 1990s yet nothing was done about it. The major mining activity in the country involves bauxite, but virtually nothing has been done here as yet, concerning environmental monitoring and control, as the costs of environmental recuperation are said to be so great. To date, it is the problem of gold mining which has been highlighted rather than bauxite mining in terms of its potential negative effects.

There has been only limited progress in coastal zone management. UNEP gave assistance for an assessment of the role played by mangrove ecosystems in economic development and shoreline protection. This project started in 1988 and was initially scheduled for completion in 1989. But a high level of staff turnover meant four different people were responsible in as many years and the project was not even completed by 1992. In general, the staff had no previous knowledge or experience of the subject. The lesson to be learned is that proper training is required, human resource development has to be addressed at an early stage and continued throughout. Very little fieldwork had been undertaken and all staff acutely felt the need for training. Efforts were made to create an interministerial committee on coastal zone management. It was formed in 1990 and included the Hydraulics division, Wildlife, Fisheries, the Forestry Commission, GAHEF and the Mahaica-Mahaicony-Abary Agricultural Development Authority. What are the lessons to be drawn? The key difficulty was the absence of a policy and programme with which to operate. All the parties had different interests. Terms of reference for the committee were discussed and drafted but never finally approved. Also, the level of representation was not sufficiently senior to make things happen. All of the different stakeholder interests had to be tabled and their constraints and opportunities laid out in relation to all of the other groups. These then had to be negotiated and the most appropriate "win-win" solutions devised and acted upon.

The work of GAHEF in forestry was limited. A consultant joined GAHEF as part of a Guyana Rainforest Sustainability Programme (GRSP). Initial funding came from the UK Open University. The GRSP had three basic aims:

- To help establish appropriate ecological conservation and forestry training programmes, encouraging local and international participation.
- To assess the feasibility of sustainable timber exploitation, while investigating the ecological impact of such exploitation.
- To carry out detailed biodiversity studies with the objective of assessing the distribution and abundance of potentially useful forest products throughout the GRSP and PSTF study area.

There was much confusion over the institutional mandate for forestry. GAHEF perceived its role as having the mandate to deal with forestry conservation and the Forestry Commission being more concerned with the commercial exploitation of timber. The GNRA, to which the Forestry Commission belonged, had a very different perspective regarding itself as being responsible for both forest industries and conservation. There was a good deal of confusion also concerning the various forestry initiatives. There was a Commonwealth and Government of Guyana *Programme for Sustainable Tropical Forestry* (PSTF), the CIDA-GOG *National Forestry Action Plan 1990-2000*, the Tropenbos initiative and the GRSP which was the only one with a GAHEF base. The lesson here is fairly obvious, clarify the mandates and give a clear lead to each institution and where potential conflicts exist create an institutional forum to broker the conflicting interests. Responsibility for the Kaieteur National Park remained confused for a long period of time, initially as between GAHEF and GNRA. Yet again the same solution was required.

Inevitably, with the change of government following the democratic elections, there was something of a policy and institutional hiatus in relation to the environment. Economic reforms took precedence.

Two years after the PPP Civic government came to power there was a significant reorganisation of institutional responsibility for the environment. The Environment Division was taken out of GAHEF in 1994 and placed in the Office of the President. This appeared to increase significantly the importance of the environment within the institutional structure of government. It was placed under Dr Lakeram Chatarpaul, the special adviser on science, technology and the environment to the President.

The next crucial development came directly as a response to the environment disaster at Omai in 1995. International aid agencies, emerging environment NGOs in Guyana and the government reacted vociferously to the event and the public profile of environment concerns was raised considerably. This was a watershed in environmental awareness. As a result of the disaster, the government moved with greater impetus and in 1996 the Environment Protection Act was passed, under which the Environment Division within the Office of the President was elevated to an Environment Protection Agency (EPA). The EPA was given considerably strengthened powers. It assumed overall responsibility for land policy. The former predominance of the GNRA in the state management of the natural resource base was thereby seriously undermined.

These moves have to be understood in the context of being part of a wider process of the new government remodelling the power structures associated with the old regime. A general trend that can be discerned was towards giving more power to the *agencies* in government. The functions of the EPA, for example, included regulation, enforcement, policy formulation, education and public awareness and research. These functions are common to the other semi-autonomous agencies of government including the GNRA, GGMC and GFC.[2]

At the time of writing in 1997, it is fair to say that the EPA was still trying to find its feet, look for staff and begin to try to put its mandate into practice. The new powers of the EPA sitting within the Office of the Presidency centralise power more and potentially raise the importance of environment concerns and the opportunity for improved coordination. The danger remains, however, that the driving imperative for short term and immediate economic development may continue to dominate over long term issues of sustainability and coordination. Yet policy formulation has been strengthened with ODA support. Under the EPA any development project with environment implications must produce an Environmental Impact Assessment for the EPA to evaluate. In addition there are efforts being made to update legislation and build capacity. Whilst being welcome, these need to be significantly reinforced.

Ministry of Agriculture

The Ministry had a number of divisions: Crops and Livestock division (which includes wildlife); Fisheries; Hydraulics division (dealing with sea defences and drainage); Lands and Surveys (which included hydrographics, the movement of mudflats along the coast); Hydrometeorology; National Agricultural Research Institute; and MMA-ADA.

Regular monthly meetings of all the divisions were held within the Ministry, hence ensuring some internal communication flow in the early 1990s. Relations were said to be good with GAHEF and GNRA. Most of the institutions remain depleted of qualified staff, however, as a result of the general economic decline and skills' exodus. A very limited research capability existed therefore, and this situation continued throughout the 1990s.

The Wildlife section of the Crops and Livestock Division is very small. Guyana is party to the CITES convention and Wildlife Services is meant to monitor and control the export of wildlife according to the convention, providing licenses to collectors and exporters of wildlife. However, at the CITES meeting in Japan in March 1992, Guyana openly acknowledged the difficulties it faced in ensuring compliance given a shortage of resources. A draft act existed but was not yet law.

Research capability here also is very limited and only one survey had been undertaken - of crocodiles in 1988 - by the early 1990s. The Wildlife services have relied heavily on estimates provided by people in the industry (not always the most reliable source) and on European Union advice. The legal export of wildlife in 1989 was valued at $2.3 million, which is quite significant in a small and ailing economy. The size of illegal exports is unknown. Wildlife services worked closely with GNRA, in particular concerning the Tropical Forest Action Plan. Only limited contacts existed with GAHEF. New effective operational linkages will need to be formed with the EPA.

Given the very limited research and operational capability of Fisheries, the division is simply obliged to join in with on-going bi-lateral or multi-lateral programmes and projects rather than take their own initiatives. The great disadvantage of this situation is that the division has never been able to set the agenda. This appears to be a more generalised problem in government. The

Fisheries division did not even have a boat in the early 1990s and effectively no monitoring capability. The coastguard has a boat, however, and very occasionally Venezuelan ships going after red snapper are pulled in. On 5 July 1996 the Coast Guard actually opened fire on a Venezuelan trawler fishing illegally in Guyanese waters and the crew were taken into custody by the police.[3] Fisheries rely upon catch and effort information for compiling their figures and the information received is only about 60% accurate. In the future regional collaboration is required and effective carrots and sticks for the fishing industry.

The Hydraulics division is responsible for sea defences, drainage and irrigation systems. Given the general limitations on the state's capacity for operational effectiveness, this department fares no better than the rest. Given privatisation of sugar and rice production appropriate partnerships are required.

The National Agricultural Research Institute's (NARI) mandate is to undertake agricultural and forestry research. The latter has not occurred to any significant effect and research to improve local agriculture has been slow to develop.

NARI had three research units which operated in two out of the five ecological zones within the country. There were two units on the coastal plain: Mon Repos, with the central laboratories and body of scientists; and Burma, mainly concerned with rice production. There was one unit at Abini in the intermediate savannas and this concentrated on research into sandy soils and operated in collaboration with CARDI.

NARI is run by a Board, hence has some flexibility but not as much as an agency, so there are difficulties in attracting staff. NARI began in 1985. Its main environmental concern was with pesticide use, trying to develop systems to reduce their use. The key research was on Integrated Pest Management (IPM). In addition to IPM, NARI has established a plant tissue culture facility. It should consider privatising and marketing its services.

Mahaica-Mahaicony-Abary Agricultural Development Authority (MMA-ADA)

This is a separate authority but falls under the Ministry of Agriculture. It controls the coastal development of West Coast Berbice and has its own Environmental Monitoring and Control Unit. The latter is involved in the training of technicians and in environmental field work and has been funded by the IDB through a non-reimbursable loan.

National Parks Commission

The National Parks Commission (NPC) was an independent body meeting once per month in the early 1990s, and composed of representatives from business, ministries, GAHEF, but not GNRA and sports. It was situated within the Ministry of Health, for historical reasons. The NPC was not represented in the early 1990s on the Environment Advisory Council nor on the Interministerial Advisory Council, neither was it on the Interministerial Committee on the Environment. The NPC had no scientific expertise and few, if any, resources with only a token staff component. The NPS was very much a voluntary body held responsible for parks when little, if anything, was being done outside of Georgetown and it relied upon the philanthropy of Mr Fernandes, the Chairman, a big businessman in Guyana and a few other people. The zoo and botanical gardens run by the NPC in Georgetown is the only operational "park". This was later renamed the Biodiversity Park.

Outside of the zoo and botanical gardens in the capital city, parks for the rest of the country seem to have been ignored with the exception of nominal legal protection for the Kaieteur National Park. Apart from an airstrip and a single woman caretaker there was no infrastructure or on-site park management. This essentially remained the situation up to the late 1990s.

A field visit to Kaieteur National Park confirmed that the former modest infrastructure was no longer functional, with nothing but the airstrip working. The World Wildlife Fund, in collaboration with the NPC and including GAHEF and the Ministry of Trade, initiated a diagnostic report on the park which was produced in March 1991. Two key problems were identified then and they still exist. There is no institution with both the authority and capacity to take effective control of the national parks. Responsibility for who was to take the lead in the Kaieteur National Park expansion proposal changed hands between NPC, GAHEF and GNRA in the early 1990s. In addition, the Tourism Desk within the Ministry of Trade claimed ultimate responsibility for all tourism affected activities. The NPC insisted that it had the responsibility constitutionally. But the influence of the voluntary body of the NPC appeared to be on the wane as the economic stakes were raised over control of the resources of the interior in the new economic dispensation. GAHEF, however, had the coordinating role for establishing the System of Protected Areas. In sum, there was confusion at the level of policy, legislation and mandates and inter-institutional planning barely yet existed. The logic of national parks remaining under the Ministry of Health as late as 1997, will escape the understanding of most observers. It seems to indicate quite strongly that there remains room for further institutional rationalisation within government.

A WWF proposal, supported by the NPC, was to expand the existing designated area for the Kaieteur National Park by 660 per cent. The GNRA opposed this in the early 1990s for fear that it might impede economic development initiatives, in particular mining and a proposed Japanese construction of a hydropower plant, under consideration at that time, on the Potaro Kuribrong Rivers known as the Amalia-Kaieteur Hydropower Development. GAHEF argued that the expansion of the park boundaries would, in fact, protect the watershed and therefore not be in opposition to the hydropower scheme. GNRA argued that in addition to the mining and hydropower interests being affected it might also impede development prospects for the Amerindian community. The Amerindian community had been given collective land entitlement claims. The park proposal included one national area and one area for traditional use only. GNRA argued that the second zoning category may impede a possible future collective Amerindian decision to move beyond traditional use to a new development initiative. Yet it would be perfectly possible to provide all of the necessary support to the Amerindian community within the national park framework, whereas uncontrolled development, as elsewhere in Amazonia, can have a very negative effect on the Amerindian community.

Twenty-one areas were proposed to have national park status, fifteen of which were included in the NEAP. These twenty-one areas were first formally proposed at Workshop '90 in Brazil. Little progress has been made subsequently. A sustainable development future for Guyana will require prioritising the national parks to encourage ecotourism plus debt relief.

Guyana Natural Resources Agency

The GNRA was established as an autonomous body under the control of an Executive Chairman. It was charged with the responsibility of developing the country's natural resources. The GNRA has under its umbrella the Guyana Geology and Mines Commission (GGMC) and the Guyana Forestry Commission (GFC). It was set up in the mid-1980s in an effort to promote economic development as a part of the major policy turn around. It was a very powerful government institution.

Prospective mining ventures had to obtain a license from the GGMC after filing a feasibility study and in principle submitting an EIA. These procedures were included in a new Mining Act but not in an Environment Act. The EIA's were originally then sent on to GAHEF for their approval prior to the license being granted. The GFC was responsible for the Timber Sales Agreement (TSA) which was introduced in the mid 1980's. It is a bankable document that gives permission to operate in an area for 15-25 years. Guidelines for practices are set out in the TSA. Each TSA was negotiated separately and a royalty was set based on, in theory, taking a forest inventory of the area. A management plan had to be submitted and approved before a TSA was agreed. A major problem for the GFC was that it lacked the capacity to carry out such inventories. GFC has subsequently received Canadian and German help to establish the Guyana Forestry Support and begin carrying out the inventorising. Significant help has also been provided by the Overseas Development Administration of the United Kingdom.

A National Forestry Action Plan 1990-2000 was proposed by the GFC and CIDA in 1989. A donors' meeting was originally scheduled to be held in November 1989 but was seriously delayed for three years. The plan was a composite of 37 projects requiring, at 1989 figures, $83 million in foreign assistance.

The GNRA acted as the focal point for the GEF *Programme for Sustainable Tropical Forestry* which was overseen by a Project Interagency Committee which included GAHEF, Foreign Affairs, Agriculture, IAST and the University of Guyana. This project emerged following the offer by President Hoyte to make available 900,000 acres of Amazonian rainforest as a pilot project under Commonwealth auspices studying sustainable utilisation. It remains unclear how, if at all, this project can be utilised to strengthen institutional capacity in Guyana, but given the relative weakness of institutions dealing with the environment, it would appear necessary to give this matter ongoing consideration.

The GGMC like the GFC also suffers from severe institutional limitations in exerting adequate control over the sector. Colchester reinforces concerns about the negative effects of the mining and a lack of capacity in government to redress this. He writes:

> The problem is that not only does the Guyana Geology and Mines Commission (GGMC) lack the biologists, toxicologists and laboratories needed to carry out a proper study of these environment problems but that there are no regulations to control the environmental impacts of mining anyway. Indeed, so feeble is the outreach of the Commission that even the regulations regarding filing claims, staking out concessions, declaring finds and paying royalties are regularly evaded.[4]

Some institutional rationalisation has taken place. Geology was moved from GNRA to GGMC. Yet still there are serious question marks over the institutional and human resource capacity to manage the sector effectively given the power and resources of the large mining companies and the remoteness from any effective government oversight of the large, medium and small mining concerns. The big issue is the division of labour with the newly empowered EPA. How can duplication of efforts be avoided?

University of Guyana

The university declined in parallel with the economy. Staff have left, student intake has fallen and facilities have deteriorated. However, some very dedicated people remain and it is the obvious place to locate environment training programmes. To this end a proposal was initiated to establish an Environment Studies Unit, as a joint initiative with the University of Utrecht in the Netherlands. This university also participated in the Tropenbos project to promote the rational utilisation of the tropical forest. An on-going project with the World Wildlife Fund exists to establish an institute for the study of biodiversity in Guyana. Collaboration and coordination between the government and the university remains weak, as in so many developing countries.

The Institute of Applied Science and Technology (IAST) is located on the university site but is independent of it. IAST has been run down, but hoped at one point to develop a pesticides monitoring unit through a UNDP/IDA institution strengthening project.

Human settlement institutions

The Central Housing and Planning Authority is responsible for overall planning for urban and human settlements. The utilities fall under the control of a number of institutions. Potable water supplies are the responsibility of the Guyana Water Authority (GUYWA). The Government Analyst has responsibility to ensure that the supply of water meets local potability standards. GUYWA has no quality control laboratory of its own however. Sewerage and sewage disposal is undertaken by the Guyana Sewerage and Water Company in Georgetown. In other urban areas the local authority is responsible for sewage disposal. No treatment takes place at present. All sewage is discharged, untreated into the sea. Solid waste disposal is the responsibility of the local authorities and, in Georgetown, the Georgetown City Council. Disposal has proved to be a major problem in the capital and a series of studies have been undertaken to devise both an immediate and long-term plan for this problem.

Non-Governmental organisations

As in the case of most societies undergoing a transition away from a state centralised socialist development practice, the organs of civil society remain fledgling and fragile. Given the absence of an awakened public consciousness about environment concerns, unsurprisingly environmental organisations are only just emerging in this final decade of the 20th century. The Guyana Biodiversity Society was formed in August 1991 and is involved in conservation and natural history. The society held monthly meetings and produced a newsletter, *The Trumpeter*. This was the only environmental NGO for a while. It was founded and run mainly by ex-patriots.

In 1992 the Guyana Environment Monitoring and Conservation Organisation (GEMCO) was formed. It rapidly assumed a fairly high profile in the local press, openly questioning the terms of agreements made by the government with foreign multinationals over natural resource exploitation in the country, particularly forestry and mining. It drew support from the university and press organs and seems likely to remain an active pressure group and local environment consulting group. It alerted public opinion to the dangers of the Omai disaster prior to the event, indicating earlier smaller impact incidents.[5] Democratisation in the 1990s has encouraged the formation of other groups representing Amerindians, the APA, AAMG, GOIP and others. Many of the greatest challenges for future sustainable development originate in the areas where the Amerindian communities live. The fragmentation of voices claiming to represent the various Amerindian communities carries the risk of a dilution of impact. A somewhat different NGO with origins in the USA, Conservation International, has established national roots in Guyanan soil. Yet overall it would be fair to say that environment issues have still to take on a strong hold in public awareness and there is, as yet, little active interest. Coping with poverty remains the main focus of people's concerns.

The challenge of intersectoral collaboration

The problem of achieving a functioning system of intersectoral collaboration is by no means specific to Guyana. Each country, however, has its own unique history in this regard and special sets of problems. We will begin by briefly examining some of the background features of the problem in Guyana, then look at recent initiatives before going on to explore a strategy for encouraging a more satisfactory process of intersectoral collaboration.

Attitudes towards the environment

Attitudes towards the environment have inevitably been shaped by history and geography. The indigenous population of Amerindians are few in number and live, in the main, in scattered groups in the densely forested interior. They are the repositories of much unwritten wisdom concerning the sustainable utilisation of forest resources. Yet their voice is little heard. The overwhelming majority of the population are relatively recent and frequently forced immigrants of African and Asian descent who live and work along the narrow coastal strip. Their historical roots are not therefore in the local environment, they are present as a result of the cruel depredations of the slave trade and indentured labour. Guyana is a truly cosmopolitan country with 51% of the population of East Indian descent, 43% of African or mixed African descent, Ameridanians represent 4% and a final 2% is made up of a mix of Portuguese, English and Chinese. In the 1970's the country had a Chinese president, a black Prime Minister and an East Asian head of the opposition.

The cultural orientation of the majority of the population is urban and outward looking to the Caribbean rather than inward looking to South America and the forested interior of Amazonia. Guyana is the only English speaking country in South America and overland communication routes to its neighbours are dreadful, relations with Venezuela are cool to say the least, and strained at times with Brazil and Surinam. Hence Guyana is isolated both linguistically and geographically within South America. However, in the 1990s immigrants from other Latin American countries have been increasing and this will have an effect over the longer term. Around 90% of the population in total live along a narrow coastal strip and there is no manifest pressure to colonise the interior. Indeed, 70% of the GDP is produced along the coast. With the exception of widespread disquiet about the deteriorating urban environment, there is a general lack of awareness and consciousness of environment issues in general. One manifestation of this is the absence of an awareness amongst decision-makers and governmental and non-governmental agencies of the potential compatibility of environment and development concerns. This can only be resolved by launching a widespread debate on the issues which will serve to educate and clarify. Civil society organisations are fragile generally in Guyana.[6] Strengthening the structures and levels of organisation of civil society will take time.

Institutional dichotomy: development versus sustainability

Effectively the country and the government "have never had to address head-on the issue of environment and development", in the words of Winston King, the former Director of GNRA.[7] Instead, institutions have emerged concerned primarily with economic development, such as the GNRA, whilst concern with environmental issues rested with a different set of institutions, initially with GAHEF, recently with the EPA, but historically also with the National Parks Commission. Reinforcing the internal dichotomy of institutions concerned with environment and others concerned with development was outside donor involvement, which tended to stress one or the other but did not, and still does not adequately integrate a sustainable development approach into their own programmes and projects. It is therefore important that in the future governmental, non-governmental and donor institutions make every effort to adopt a more integrated sustainable development approach.

Development cooperation

In the poorest countries development cooperation inevitably plays a significant role in the economy. As a result of the government's policies, development assistance to Guyana in the 1980s was severely curtailed. Only with the move away from state control of the economy and towards democratisation did the aid flow significantly escalate in the 1990s. The top five donors in 1990 (in order) were the EU, Venezuela, the Inter American Development Bank, Canada and the USA, accounting in total for 91% of donor finance.

When the new government of President Jagan came to power it was quick to assure potential investors that it was seeking to create the right climate to encourage their participation in the country's development. The government announced its major development projects for which it was seeking finance as sea defence reconstruction ($ 191.6 million), renewing electricity supply system ($ 115 million), housing ($ 35 million) and other projects in health care, water supply, education and airport and bridge repairs.

As significant or even more significant than new investment and aid money coming into the country for long term sustainable development is finding ways of relieving the country's enormous debt burden. The new government had considerable success in obtaining debt relief. The British government agreed to a substantial debt write-off. In May 1993 the Paris Club also agreed to a significant package of debt write-off and rescheduling.

On the whole, it has to be said that the donor community needs to play a more proactive role in the future to encourage the integration of environment and development concerns in such a way as to promote a more sustainable development future. If we look at Table 1 and the sectoral distribution of aid in 1990, the environment does not even appear as a category. Virtually all of the expenditure in the natural resources category went on mineral exploration and exploitation. This would not have been so much of a problem if, within the sectors mentioned, due consideration was given to environmental concerns but this was not the case. Of the US $97.018 million external assistance in 1990, 49% was investment project assistance and 42% programme/budgetary aid or balance of payments support.

It is important to learn the lessons of the past in order to improve on future performance. This is particularly important in relation to aid programmes in a poor and highly aid dependent country such as Guyana. If we look at the record of the major aid donors in Guyana then there are positive and negative experiences. Both are potentially equally valuable, but only if the lessons are properly learnt and the necessary adjustments are made in the future aid programmes.

Hence under an original sea defences rehabilitation management plan commissioned by the EU in 1989, environmental issues were not even included in the original terms of reference of the study. In 1993 a US$ 37 million sea defence programme was finally announced involving four major multilateral aid donors, the EU, IDB, WB and CDB and an environmental study was at least under consideration. Coordination is so important, not least to avoid unnecessary duplication of efforts and the wasting of scarce development resources. For example, both the EU and the UNDP had undertaken similar studies of mangroves in the late 1980s. A single study would have sufficed a fact recognised in retrospect by both organisations. Piecemeal project initiatives are not a satisfactory substitute for overall coastal zone planning.

Of course, the donors are constrained by the extent to which the government is prioritising an integrated sustainable development approach. Hence donors have continued to act with scepticism over the NFAP which was widely regarded as being more concerned with timber exploitation rather than effective conservation of forest resources.

Sustainability through the window of development

The protracted decline in the economy over the 1980's culminated in the adaptation of a structural adjustment policy and an end to socialist development efforts. A renewed free market led development initiative is now underway. The whole climate is one of encouraging private development initiatives, with restoring economic growth the top priority concern. This is, of course, understandable and commendable given the dramatic economic decline that had occurred.

What this means is that sustainability and concern with the environment will only be taken seriously when addressed through the window of development. New initiatives must look to the development imperative but show how environmental concerns can be addressed to enhance development efforts. As the former Executive Director of GNRA observed, "We cannot deplete our resources today to make development more difficult in the future."[8]

Given the imperative of economic growth, environmental issues can be seen as being merely an impediment to this process. It can be regarded as an unnecessary additional cost that may act as a disincentive for investment. Concretely, the government might be asked to carry out an EIA on a proposed project which may lead to it being rejected and the government will then be left with no option other than paying the bill for the EIA.

Improving institutional coordination

Overall, environment institutions in Guyana as they have evolved over the years were set up essentially as a monitoring and control entity whereas the key functions needed to be education and coordination. Institutional strengthening is required in these latter two areas in particular, in addition to improving a capacity for monitoring and control. By strengthening the government's capacity for coordination and education, impetus will be given to improving overall interagency cooperation and to strengthening the institutions of civil society who need to be the partners with government of sustainable development initiatives.

The institutional set-up to date has reinforced a conflictual model between environment and development concerns. This was exacerbated by the *de facto* reporting structures under the Hoyte government. The Executive Director of GAHEF reported directly to the Prime Minister's office, not through a ministry. However, with the introduction of a programme of structural adjustment within the country, the office of the Prime Minister was abolished when the number of ministries was reduced from 18 to 11. Fortuitously the Prime Minister at the time was also Minister of Health, which provided the continuing reporting link to GAHEF.

Constitutionally power is very much centred on the Presidency and the subsequent changes appear to have weakened the office of the Prime Minister and strengthened those of the Presidency. Following the death in office of President Jagan in 1997 it remains unclear what future dispensation with emerge. It is essential to ensure that the centralisation of the environment mandate within the Presidency is never used to simply rubber stamp any economic development initiative that comes across a busy desk.

An early structure to encourage interagency cooperation concerning environmental issues was the Environmental Advisory Council (EAC) with public and private sector membership. Those who attended include GNRA, Agriculture, Trade and Tourism, the Water Authority, Guyana Mines, Housing but not the University. Representation was at a low level. Initially the Advisory Council met once per month but subsequently meetings were held more infrequently. Currently there is a National Resources Advisory Board which includes GNRA, GFC, GGMC, the University and NGOs. There is also a National Biodiversity Committee and with UNDP support this body has presented a national plan which has gone to cabinet for consideration.

Within the original National Environmental Strategy, interagency coordination was meant to operate by each Ministry or Agency appointing a focal point with whom GAHEF would liaise concerning all matters related to the national environmental programme. The Ministry/Agency Focal Point (MAFP) might or might not have been the same representative who attended the EAC. The role of the MAFP was stated to be

-    To coordinate the input of their Ministry/Agency and any other institutions/organisations for whom they are responsible into the programme;
-    To maintain close links with the GAHEF.

National institutions and government departments would be designated by ministries to provide the institutional base for specific activities. Where required, networking would enable different institutions to participate. The difficulty with this proposed structure was that for intersectoral cooperation to work there had to be a policy making level of coordination. That became possible in theory with the introduction of the Interagency Committee on the Environment in the latter part of 1991. This committee, chaired by GAHEF, could potentially have taken decisions and ensure that a lead was given for genuine intersectoral collaboration. Relatively junior level MAFP's reporting directly to GAHEF could never have ensured the necessary level of influence to help overcome the potentially immense institutional constraints to successfully implementing a NEAP. The EAC never had the weight to ensure this either.

The limitation with the EAC was that it was advisory to GAHEF only, the level of representation was too low and it had no authority or mandate to direct interministerial coordination. An important potential step forward came in September 1991 when the Cabinet authorised the formation of an Interagency Committee on the Environment with representatives of ministries and agencies from Permanent Secretary or Chief Technical Officer level up to the Ministers. GAHEF chaired this committee, was the coordinating agency and provided the secretariat. This was a policy level structure with the power to call on any body to participate.

Meetings of this committee held in 1992, were attended by the Prime Minister, Minister of Agriculture, Special Advisory to the President on Foreign Affairs and the heads of GAHEF and GNRA. The Interagency Committee only included governmental representatives. The EAC, with its governmental and non-governmental representatives, would advise the Interagency Committee.

The formation of a policy-making body, the Interagency Committee on the Environment, marked a further step forward in laying the foundations for enhanced intersectoral coordination. For such a committee to function effectively, however, a clear mandate had to be established and agreed by all parties.

In addition, further thought and clarification was required concerning the mandates of the existing institutions dealing with environment and development issues. These institutions had been set up with a conflictual model in mind. There were some institutions with a development mandate and others with an environmental conservation mandate. Whilst this provided one institutional model of how environment and development concerns and the potential conflicts over resource use could be handled, it was not the only model, nor was it necessarily the most appropriate one. On the eve of the next millennium, these issues still remain to be resolved.

Whilst monitoring and control mechanisms will always be required, very little effort seems at present to go into openly discussing in an appropriate forum and publicly, potential resource conflicts and how these might be reconciled through improved natural resource management. Such discussions could help: develop a policy consensus; build institutional capacity; encourage interagency cooperation; educate and 'raise awareness of the issues; and encourage widespread participation.

An effective National Environmental Action Programme will only be able to move forward if the political will, and legislative and institutional format is put in place to make it happen. Otherwise, Guyana will not be able to take the international lead in this regard, which it is so well-placed to assume. Finally, it is necessary to draw out the lessons from the earlier institutional history in order to shape a more appropriate institutional framework for the future. This chapter has attempted to outline some of this institutional history which might otherwise have been forgotten. There has been one glaring omission in the discussion to date and that is deliberate. The whole question of improving the human resource management of the natural resource base must involve a serious measure of decentralisation. This is a major challenge which will be addressed in the following chapter.

Notes

1.   This chapter relies heavily for the institutional history upon interviews carried out in 1992 with most of the key actors in the institutions discussed in the text and an enormous debt of gratitude is due to all of the people who gave so generously of their time. Special thanks are due to Dr Walter Chin and all of the staff of GAHEF and the Environment Division, in particular Bridget Bouell. Thanks are also due to the staff on UNDP, in particular Thomas Gittens. A special word of thanks is due to Patrick Williams of UNDP for his kindness and wisdom in updating me on a rapidly changing institutional context in the late 1990s.

2.   P. Williams, *Institutional Framework for Land Management in Guyana*, a paper given at the conference on Environment and Development in Guyana, Centre for Developing Areas Research, Royal Holloway, University of London, 7 May 1997.

3.   *Guyana Review*, No 47, December 1996, p.4.

4.   M. Colchester, "Guyana: Fragile Frontier", *Race and Class*, Vol 38, No 4, 1997, p.40.

5.   P. Williams *op cit*.

6.   See T. Ferguson, *Structural Adjustment and Good Governance: The Case of Guyana*, Public Affairs Consulting Enterprise, Georgetown, 1995.

7.   Interview with Winston King, Director of GNRA, Georgetown, January 1992.

8.   Interview with Winston King *op cit*.

10 Reviewing progress in the 1990s

Undeniably, Guyana's prospects had considerably improved over the 1990s as a result of policy reform and democratisation. It is heartening to report, at the macroeconomic level, a steady improvement across many of the key economic indicators (see Table 1).

Most impressive are the rates of real GDP growth, improving steadily from 6% in 1991 to 8.5% in 1994. Whilst dropping slightly in 1995 and 1996, growth still remained between 5% and 7% in these two years. According to the Economist Intelligence Unit, the likelihood is that in 1997 and 1998 it will be higher still.[1] By the mid 1990s, GDP per capita, according to some studies, had risen to $ 510.[2] Inflation has been brought under control. It has dropped from an annual rate of 80% in 1991 to 8.1% in 1995. The debt service ratio has dropped over the same period from 35% to under 20%. These represent real gains in terms of macroeconomic indicators.

After the decades of stagnation and decline the economic upturn will be welcomed. Yet there are dangers that the dash for growth may be at the expense of caution. The temptation to sell off rapidly to foreign investors rights for the commercial utilisation of the natural resources is understandable. Foreign investment and management is desperately needed, it will bring economic growth and the benefits will slowly filter down to the wider population. Yet safeguards are required if the upside of this investment and growth is to be maximised. The potential downside is a free-for-all in which environmental and social safeguards are forfeited. These can produce a nasty negative reaction which can set-back the prospects of longer term, sustainable development. Serious inequality can breed crime, social instability and this can be a powerful deterrent to investors. Environmental tragedies can have serious humanitarian effects but also impede effective multisectoral usage of a common resource base.

A number of set-backs to an overall picture of steady growth and development serve as an important warning of what can happen when some of the crucial environment and development challenges identified in this monograph are not seriously addressed.

Table 1
Sectoral distribution of aid to Guyana (1990)

Sector	Financing (US $m)
International Trade	31.807
Natural Resources	15.531
Agriculture	10.843
Area Development	10.195
Industry	7.212
Energy	6.899
Human Resources	5.450
Health	3.299
Development Admin	3.001
Social Development	1.961
Economic Management	0.612
Transport	0.128
Domestic Trade	0.072
Communication	0.008
	97.018

Source: UNDP, Development Cooperation Guyana Report, 1990

Environmental warnings

The first of these relates to the mining sector. Two years after President Jagan opened the Omai Gold Mine early in 1993 with the words "We're turning a mud land into a gold land!", he declared that the spillage of millions of gallons of dam waters at the plant containing cyanide, sediment and biologically active wastes into the Omai and Essequibo rivers as being "the country's worst environmental disaster".[3] Whilst in retrospect, this spectre of gloom may not have been realised in practice the threat was no less real. The company's public relations comment that it was merely "an industrial accident", as reported internationally, did nothing to allay potential fears.[4] For three days the contents of the tailings pond of the massive Omai gold mine poured into the rivers. As far as is currently known, there were no short term human fatalities, although there was ample evidence of fish dying and even some livestock.[5] What is not in doubt, is that production in the Omai mine was suspended as a result of the spill seriously affecting the country's overall economic growth.

A second environmental warning involved the flooding in 1996, which highlighted the continuing inadequacies in coastal zone management and flood controls. An estimated 30,000 people were affected, who received food and medicines, and emergency dredging work had to be undertaken.[6]

According to Halcrow, the risk of flooding in Greater Georgetown has increased for the following reasons:

-   An increase in impervious areas
-   Infilling of drains
-   Maintenance failure of existing drainage
-   Refuse disposal in existing drains
-   Lack of secondary and roadside drainage systems
-   Squatters settling on drainage reserves
-   A relative rise in the sea level
-   Uncontrolled urban expansion into unserviced areas[7]

According to Mark Pelling's important new research, a greater flood risk is combined with increased human vulnerability to flood as a result of economic frailty, poor governance and institutional collapse.[8] He highlights 21 floods identified by the press in Georgetown between January 1990 and June 1996. On the basis of a vulnerability assessment involving interviews with 232 households sampled from four case study neighbourhoods he draws the following conclusions.[9] Vulnerability results from: lack of development of community organisations; inadequate household adaptation; inadequate access to household economic resources; particular demographic household characteristics; inadequate access to secure housing; inadequate domestic service provision; and inadequate access to necessary and affordable health care.

Pelling identifies the vulnerable groups including low income households, small-scale agriculturalists, single female households, children, renters, squatters and bottom house dwellers (many houses are built off the ground and people live also on the ground floor underneath the main house). Whilst people are in some degree proactive in their adaptive responses to the flooding through raising yards, some local environment improvement and so on, Pelling identifies key institutional weaknesses. The first relate to Georgetown. Vulnerability to flooding here is heightened by a weak civil society which stifles community organisations, there are conflicts between national and city government, which are dominated by different political groupings and finally gaps exist in support mechanisms for CBOs. Hence, for example, under the SIMAP quango funding programme, urban areas are not included in its remit, neither are the squatter areas. In the peri-urban areas institutional challenges are no less apparent. The Community Development Councils have become heavily politicised and captured by local political elites, hence no longer represent the most vulnerable groups, there are also tensions with the local authorities and between funding agencies and the local community. This leads us on directly to the problem of decentralisation and coordination.

Decentralisation and coordination

Decentralisation, improving local resource management and improving institutional coordination are a package of issues which could help to ensure a more sustainable development future but which appear far from finding any satisfactory resolution at present. Local democratic institutions and local government in Guyana is ineffectual and chaotic. In 1994 there were the first democratic local council elections since 1970. Previously opposition parties boycotted local elections as a protest against national electoral fraud. Local government was effectively in the hands of central government appointees in the form of mayors and district councillors. The overall economic decline was reflected in an increasingly skeletal and ineffective local government system. It was in sum, a totally top-down inoperational model.

The country was divided into ten administrative regions in 1980. Only in 1990, however, was the system of 129 neighbourhood democratic councils (NDCs) introduced. In 1994 only half of the NDCs were opened up for elections, with the government deeming that population levels were inadequate to warrant setting up councils in the remaining districts.

The weaknesses of central government are magnified yet further when it comes to local government. The Ministry of Public Works, Communication and Regional Development (PWC&RD) has central government responsibility for local government. In early 1995 for example, PWC&RD had only one out of seven local government staff positions filled and funds allocated to RDCs rarely reach the interior.[10]

In order to better represent local authority interests a National Congress of Local Democratic Organs (NCLDO) was legally established in 1980. This replaced the former Guyana Association of Local Authorities which appears to have been relatively effective as a non partisan watchdog of central government. In contrast, the NCLDO has been completely ineffectual. It has no resources, not even a telephone and it only met once over the period from the elections in 1992 to 1995. The institution was clearly on its last legs.

Regional Democratic Councils (RDCs) exist in all ten regions of the country. They exist to carry out central government policy and do not have the capacity to create policy based upon specific regional needs. RDCs supervise

NDCs. RDCs depend upon central funding allocations, whilst retaining authority for small-scale fundraising. In practice, central funding covers salaries and minimal operating costs. Any genuine development initiatives depend upon separate project funding. The key professional link- person between the RDC and NDC is the district development officer.

Problems are legion and have been identified by the Washington based National Democratic Institute for International Affairs (NDIIA) as follows.[11] There is no common understanding between elected representatives and local government officials of their respective roles. There is no clear demarcation of jurisdictions between RDCs and NDCs, neither is there a legal framework outlining the relationship between the two. Unsurprisingly, the actual relationship on the ground varies enormously from one region to another.

Most worrying of all in the words of the NDIIA report is that: "The lack of communication and confusion of roles have led to an extraordinarily low level of integration of development plans between the regional and neighbourhood levels."[12] This lack of spatial coordination is further complicated as it is refracted by political expediencies. RDCs dominated by one party will not be inclined to support NDCs ruled by opposing parties. Similarly, the political flavour of the national government will predispose which RDCs will be favoured in resource allocation.

Nine out of the ten regions have NDCs. Their responsibilities include maintaining roads and bridges, garbage collection, playgrounds and day-care centres as well as tax collection, licensing fees, market operations and rent collection. Yet as soon as we review the realities of resource allocation then the limitations of local government capacity becomes all too apparent. Central government grants to NDCs range between US$ 700 and 2,000. This is peanuts. In theory NDCS will raise their own revenues from property taxes, but as property assessments have not been completed and operationalised, in effect all is dependent on central grants. The NDCs are obliged to formulate budgets based upon a 100% rate of tax collection whilst the reality is that only 25% to 30% of tax is collected.

NDCs are obliged to create standing committees on finance and public works. They can also create committees on health, the environment and land distribution. Whilst committees have been created they are not very effective. There is little public participation in council meetings. NDCs remain subordinate to central government.

Community Development Councils (CDCs) have no legal standing but emerged in the late 1980s as vehicles to implement hardship mitigation projects associated with the Economic Recovery Plan -the Social Impact Amelioration Programme. CDCs operate within NDCs and under their approval. Eventually the CDCs may be absorbed within the NDCs. The NDIIA report highlights the problem of potential conflict of interests as a person may be the Chair of an NDC and of a CDC seeking NDC approval for development initiatives. There is also the on-going likelihood that CDCs become politicised.

The NDIIA report concludes as follows:

> The central government and national political parties have paid scant attention to the development of local government in Guyana. Despite the growing public enthusiasm for meaningful, accessible governance, the confusion of roles and responsibilities, the lack of council autonomy, and absence of formal training opportunities have all contributed to the inability of the government to provide adequate services. In addition, the continuing financial vulnerability of local government entities and the absence of trained and professional government officials have led to a lack of public confidence in local government, which continues today.[13]

Sustainable development will require a more effective structure of democratically accountable local government with some decentralisation of power. The Minister of PWC&RD can at present arbitrarily overturn local government decisions.

Poverty and social welfare

There is an enormous social welfare challenge facing the country. When meeting the basic needs of society is applied as a yardstick to assess development progress in Guyana, there is clearly still a very long way to go. The first real difficulty is obtaining accurate and credible data, although intuitive, impressionistic and anecdotal data abound. Studies that do exist are to be commended heartily, for trying to lift a veil of ignorance on part of the picture at least. Too often, though, writers may remain ill-served by the theoretical or other form of narrow research optic employed, and may be constrained in particular, by the specific nature of commissioned sectoral research, which does not allow one to gain a true overall picture. All those who have contributed to the research endeavour on the country are to be congratulated, as they do not have an easy task, yet still we remain with a somewhat vague and impressionistic picture of the social welfare challenge. The macro economic data does not add up convincingly to provide a comprehensive account of how the real economy operates and the information offered in survey data by families, does not equate either to the obvious successful survival of most people.

This serves to reinforce the importance of sustainable livelihood thinking as a central tenet of sustainable development. We need to understand how in practice people sustain their livelihoods. On this basis, development initiatives to serve the poor can be targeted. In fact when we probe into the best of the research we can begin to uncover some of this reality. Linda Peake's work on poverty in Linden, the second largest town in the country, is revealing.[14] Her focus, usefully, is actually on household coping mechanisms in the era of structural adjustment. Whilst most women surveyed conveyed a sense that they were continuing to suffer from on-going economic crises, what is most heartening, is that the majority of households have successfully adopted coping mechanisms. These involve diversifying sources of income, engaging in waged work and restructuring household management. The first such mechanism tends to befuddle researchers working in Guyana. Essentially, foreign remittances in one form or another are a vital survival mechanism for what may be called a labour reserve economy in the global economic system. Guyana provides a serious brain drain and skilled labour subsidy to the world economy. There is, however, a payback, via remittances. These are not by any means always recorded - they are dollars, offer of accommodation or a thousand other inputs returned to families still resident in Guyana by the very many migrants.

Internally, wage earning opportunities have been switching from the formal to the informal sector, in the main into commerce and the service sector. Given the constraints of the state socialist legacy, for some time to come it is likely that informal sector earnings will exceed formal sector state salaries. This should have all kinds of policy ramifications in terms of the shaping of education and human resource development policy and in the nature of poverty alleviation programmes for self-help.

Karl Bennett's comparative study of economic decline and the growth of the informal sector in Guyana and Jamaica is revealing.[15] His study analyses data for the period 1977 to 1989 and demonstrated that official statistics on income which exclude the informal sector significantly understate true income levels. Yet estimating the size of the informal sector is extremely difficult. Clive Thomas suggests for the period 1982 to 1986 estimates for the informal sector vary from a low of 26% to a high of 99% of GDP, but on average it was well in excess of 50% of GDP.[16] Looking at comparable related studies, Bennett confirms that an estimate of informal income amounting to around 50% of reported income appears to be reasonable.[17]

Ascertaining the overall significance of the informal sector is not sufficient to deduce that the poorer and more marginalised members of society were actually the ones to benefit from the vitality of the informal sector. Indeed, in the context of a "norm of illegality", in Clive Thomas' memorable phrase, rejection of a corrupt state authority in the context of economic decline meant that most if not nearly all people were engaged in some degree in the informal economy.[18] Moreover, Bennett's research suggests that an increase in the value of goods and services produced by the informal sector did not necessarily mean that marginalised groups were benefiting: "On the contrary, there is evidence to suggest that the expansion of the informal sector was a reflection of the relatively successful efforts of more privileged groups ... to maintain their income levels and traditional patterns of consumption."[19] In a reflective piece relatively early on in the experience of Guyana's structural adjustment programme, Thomas indicates that as a result of the programme the parallel economy had shrunk to about 19% of the official economy by the early 1990s.[20] One would expect this trend to continue, with what was once the informal now becoming the formal sector as state socialism is replaced by the free market.

Women in particular carry the heavy burden of poverty on their shoulders. Interestingly whilst women from the Caribbean generally have higher participation rates in the labour force compared with women from other developing countries, general worker rates for women were lowest in Guyana at 20% for all of the Commonwealth Caribbean (1980 figures), rising to a high of 55% in the British Virgin Islands.[21] With formal sector employment opportunities restricted, Guyanese women inevitably turned to the informal sector. Women traders in Guyana's informal sector export local products and import basic commodities:

Guyanese traders, for example, sell locally manufactured gold jewellery, garments and straw baskets in neighbouring territories and buy food, drugs and school supplies to sell at home.[22]

Winners and losers?

Tyrone Ferguson has produced an interesting and important analysis of the early effects of structural adjustment and good governance criteria as these have impacted upon Guyana.[23] The most significant findings of his study relate to his investigation of the impact on the political economy of the country of the structural adjustment as it relates to winner and loser groups. These are outlined in Table 2.

Table 2

**Profile of winners/losers under structural adjustment by broad categories
of interest groups**

	Economic Interest Groups	Racial Groups	Geographical Groups	Public/Private Sectors	Political Groups
Winners	Business Agriculture	East Indian Portuguese	Rural	Private	Opposition Political Parties
Losers	Public Sector Labour	African Amerindian	Urban Hinterland	Public	Ruling Party*

* Former ruling PNP party

Source: Ferguson, 1996

If we take this table to be broadly representative of the categories of key stakeholders, with certain reservations about his column of geographical groups being too generalised, then we need to ask the question what does this mean for future sustainable development prospects? Here we probably have to distinguish first of all the development dynamic of growth from both the redistributive and equity dimensions and conservation of the environment.

In terms of the economic dynamic, there was no viable alternative at this time to a move away from the state centred to the private sector led development model, as the former had demonstrably failed after more than two decades of implementation. Ironically in Guyana, both government and opposition had championed the state led model and both were undergoing a profound readjustment of policy focus. In both the Hoyte and the subsequent Jagan government the tension was visible between the old, state-centred habits of a lifetime and the new imperatives. Inevitably there would be ambiguities and an uneven application of the structural adjustment package. However, both the Hoyte and Jagan governments have demonstrated a determination for it to succeed.

Interestingly what is missing from the very useful table by Ferguson, is a breakdown of the external and internal business interests. It would be interesting to examine the winners and the losers in relation to foreign and domestic private sectors. Inevitably this will be an on-going saga.

But let us take each of the columns in turn. First of all we have economic interest groups. The winners are given as business and agriculture and the losers as the public sector and labour. On the positive side, business and agriculture stakeholder groups can have the freedom to pursue economic growth strategies. Being successful they will produce wealth and employment. Losers are primarily the public sector. Hence the first question becomes "has the public sector become so weakened that it can neither establish, monitor or enforce the necessary guidelines and regulations to ensure the sustainable management of the natural resource base?". If the weakening of the public sector proceeds so far that the prospects of anything other than a free-for-all mining of the natural resources of the country appears slim, then development is unlikely to be sustainable.

In terms of labour, by which it is assumed to mean organised labour, then its formerly privileged position in a quasi-corporativist arrangement no longer remains. The big question here concerns the longer term and how to raise the skills level of the labour force to compete globally. This is exactly the problem which is currently being tackled in South Africa.

The biggest long term social and political problem remains the complete racial polarisation of the electoral process. The winners of the racial groups are the East Indian and Portuguese communities and the losers are the African and possibly the Amerindian communities. In essence once the African community was hit by the dual blow of its representative political party losing power and the switch from a public sector model of development dominated by Afro-Guyanese employment, to a private sector model dominated by indigenous Indo-Guyanese capital then the die was cast for tough times ahead for the Afro-Guyanese community.

In the case of Guyana, the pre-reform authoritarian political model guaranteed an Afro-Guyanese minority dominance, whilst democracy appears to guarantee an Indo-Guyanese majority race rule into the foreseeable future. The problem with such a scenario is that it raises the all too common spectre of the creation of a permanent underclass. Rising criminality is the threat in all such similar circumstances around the globe, in South Africa, Mexico and so many other countries.

What are the prospects for building a more sustainable development future for Guyana? David Kaimowitz has indicated three main determinants of environmental policy reform in Latin America: the relative degree of power of groups favouring and opposing reforms; the compatibility of reforms with the prevailing economic development models; and finally the institutional capacity to implement the reforms.[24] He identifies seven distinct groups which have prompted environment concerns on the continent:

i)   Developed country organisations (multilateral, bilateral and NGO)
ii)   Middle class environmental organisations
iii)   Entrepreneurs involved in green business

iv)   Farmers and communities affected by pollution
v)   Indigenous communities
vi)   Professional environmentalists
vii) Political parties and social movements concerned with social justice.

Over all seven categories, Guyana does not fare too well. Undeniably, outside concerns with the environment have played a big role within Latin American in general and in the specific case of Guyana. The poverty of the country, the richness of its forests and biodiversity and the considerable influence of multilateral, bilateral and NGO aid organisations have combined to give a considerable weight to the concerns of this group, reflecting the higher levels of environmental awareness in North America and Europe. We have seen how these groups have become involved in a number of initiatives in Guyana. However, it is fair to say that the international community has been quite slow to encourage the integration of environment and development concerns. Hence in the original terms of reference for the massive programme to recuperate the sea defences in 1989 environmental issues were not included. Tables produced in 1990 on the sectoral distribution of aid did not even include the environment as a separate category and virtually all of the expenditure in the natural resources category went on mineral exploration and exploitation.[25] *Per se* this would not necessarily be a problem, if within the sectors due consideration was given to environment concerns.

There are indications that concern and active interest is growing within the donor community. Yet much more effort is required to coordinate initiatives. Hence both the UNDP and European Union carried out a similar study of mangroves. With aid resources becoming ever more scarce it is important to avoid such duplication of efforts.

The urban middle class is small in Guyana. In neighbouring Brazil in 1989 there was 700 environmental organisations mostly based in the cities of the prosperous south east.[26] The small population of Guyana, the extensive emigration of its skilled middle class over decades and the overall poverty and isolation of the country have impeded the development of such groups. Also the extremes of urban environmental pollution of Mexico City and Sao Paulo are far removed from the context of Georgetown. Yet environmental awareness will grow. The current economic upturn will benefit primarily the middle class and exposure to these issues through the global and local media will produce over time a more vocal lobby, not least as a response to incidents such as that at Omai goldmine. Indeed with the decline of the left-right ideological struggles of previous decades, environment and sustainable development are replacing the previous rallying cries of marxism and radical socialism in many parts of the world. The difficulty appears to be sustaining the momentum of middle class interest and involvement.

The next four groups are motivated by direct material interests. First are those individuals and companies producing for a "green" market. In Guyana this involves a number of tourist enterprises engaged in travel to the interior and accommodation amongst other concerns. Production of organic foods and of sustainably managed products have a growing global market. These avenues will increasingly be explored by entrepreneurs and producers driven by a growing market demand. Guyana has a long way to go to catch up with Chile, Costa Rica and Ecuador in ecotourist development, but the potential is there and being the only English speaking country in Latin America it is well positioned to take advantage of North American and wider global market demand.

A very different group is those negatively affected by pollution. In Guyana these would include fishermen on the rivers and inshore coastal waters, agricultural workers in rice and sugar production who may have their health affected by toxic pesticides, miners placed at risk by mercury and cyanide in the production process. Given the shortage of formal sector employment generally, effective action will require enlightened employer practices encouraged by government legislation, support and monitoring and where applicable a union awareness of the salient issues and a prioritising of these in negotiations with management.

Indigenous peoples have had an uphill struggle to protect their forest home and retain the land rights necessary to preserve their way of life. Amerindian communities in Guyana have had nothing like the publicity accorded to the Yanomami Indians in Brazil for example. They are still struggling to make their voice heard. Unfortunately in the late 1990s that voice has become very fragmented thereby diminishing its effectiveness. A proliferation of NGOs were emerging claiming to represent the Amerindian community.

Professional environmentalists are a very small group in Guyana. But again, one can expect to see this as a group which will grow over time. It includes lecturers, journalists, staff in NGO and governmental agencies. What it lacks in size it can often make up for in influence.

There is most definitely an upsurge of publications on environment issues in the 1990s, often associated with the formation of new groups such as the Association of Guyanese Environmental Media.[27] How to look after the environment and also ensure development manuals began to appear on such issues as agroforesty.[28] Whilst some new publications coming out of Georgetown had a narrow focus on Guyana, others adopted a wider Caribbean perspective.[29] The University also produced valuable studies on sustainable development issues.[30]

As global concerns and market opportunities expand in terms of environment issues, there will be ever greater incentives for the above groups to grow. In essence, when "sustainability" becomes a means of sustaining livelihoods, sustainable development becomes the collective beneficiary of individual self-motivations.

All of the above indigenously grounded groups are not major forces across the Latin American continent in general, and in Guyana in particular for reasons of history and isolation their effects are even further reduced. Donor efforts can help nurture such concerns and need to be seriously addressed.

The final group identified by Kaimovitz is movements for social justice including political parties. Women's political organisations certainly have a considerable history in Guyana, yet various factors have limited the impact of women's political organisations on women's liberation.[31] Women's groups were often subordinate to the two main political parties. Women's own struggles were subordinated, in the language of the time, to national liberation and socialist struggles. Out of one of the smaller more radical political parties, the Working People's Alliance (WPA) there emerged a small but dynamic women's organisation that was very proactive, called Red Thread.[32]

Whilst the forces potentially in support of environmental policy reform are fragile and sometimes only embryonic, the forces pulling in the other direction appear all too powerful. Multi-national companies and local elites in the poorest of countries have only their natural resource base to exploit. Hence mining, forestry and fishing are just three of the ways in which profit can be made from the land and water resources of a country. The tendency is to exploit the non-renewable resources as quickly as possible through the granting of mining and timber concessions and to overstretch the use of renewable resource such as the forests and fish to maximise short term benefits at the expense of ensuring that the stock of the resource is adequately renewed. Eating into the capital stock inevitably results in a diminishing long term yield.

How far environment policy reform is compatible with the prevailing economic models was the second determinant. The entire thrust of the current economic orthodoxy is to privatise, encourage foreign investment and develop through an export led open economy. Doors are flung open and environmental safeguards may be regarded as yet more impediments to economic growth. Large mining and timber companies and major agricultural and industrial producers wield considerable influence. For governments economic growth is the key and all too often this may ride hand in hand with personal enrichment. In sum, there is every reason to regard the possibility of environment policy reform somewhat sceptically in Latin America, but no less so in Africa and Asia.

119

Structural adjustment programmes have a negative effect in the short term at least on the poor with cost recovery programmes being introduced for education, for example. Poverty places day to day concerns of survival above longer term considerations of sustainability for the majority of people. The golden rule of structural adjustment is "earn more and spend less". For governments this invariably means reducing government expenditure and cutting back on the state. Hence the administration's capacity to regulate and monitor the effects of development on the environment may be seriously impeded. Generally, such a capacity has not been very active within the state apparatus. At a time of fiscal constraint, therefore, two countervailing tendencies are required against the prevailing orthodoxy. The first of these is building up and reinforcing yet another state structure, but this time for the environment. Secondly, to be effective, this environment body relies on the cooperation of other state institutions if it is to make an impact and coordinate government response. This will be hard to achieve when even the core activities of the various branches of government are under threat from cuts and rationalisation exercises.

The turn from centralised state planning to the free market leads to a haemorrhage of talent from the state to the private sector. This invariably weakens the state's capacity for planning and implementation.

The third and final consideration is the extent of institutional capacity to implement environment reforms. Kaimowitz argues that policy-makers and bureaucrats who have a measure of autonomy from business interests may be more amenable to environment policy reforms. His checklist does not appear to place Guyana in a positive light in this regard. A large economy diminishes the impact of any one particular company or sector's interests. Guyana's economy is very small. Government does not have substantial economic resources of its own, major social upheavals have not forced business interests to make the space for popular participation in civil society. Hence the Mexican government can close down a petroleum refinery in the capital city because of pollution and the Brazilian government can abolish livestock subsidies to restrain forest destruction because the overall cost of such measures is balanced by other forces. Honduras has not the same freedom in relation to toxic pesticide use in banana plantations or Ecuador to control the environmental destruction of its mining industry. Yet the new government in Guyana had the courage to close the Omai mine after the spill.

Debt dependency severely limits governmental room for manoeuvre. This is an ambiguous situation in relation to environment policy reform. It increases the leverage of external donor actors who have a more advanced environmental global agenda precisely as a result of their own affluence, earlier internal environmental destruction and awareness of the long term negative effect this has and media awareness of global environmental issues amongst their electorates and politicians. Yet at the heart of structural adjustment is an on-going tension between the predominant economic growth and pay back your borrowings imperative, in uneasy harness with all of the policy aspirations for environmental concerns, poverty alleviation, gender awareness and so on.

Do democratisation and decentralisation inevitably increase the prospect of sustainable development? Munslow and Ekoko urge some caution in this regard in their survey of the global literature.[33]

Across the Latin American continent as a whole and we would argue, very relevant to the specific circumstances of Guyana are the following serious problems in achieving significant progress concerning environment policy reform. Firstly, there are two separate agendas which have to be brought together. Kaimowitz refers to this as the "difficulties involved in linking environmental issues with concerns for social justice".[34] It is our central thesis that it is only by linking these two concerns that countries of the South will take seriously this policy agenda and rightly so given their circumstances. It is not an easy policy synthesis to engineer. Yet it is both possible and desirable.

Existing economic orthodoxy prioritises weakening the public sector and doing everything possible to increase exports. This often means in practice mining the natural resource base for timber, minerals, fish and exotic species for export. Multinational corporations call the shots in natural resource exploitation and small fragile governments of the South have few bargaining chips. Yet they need to develop their capacity to bargain with the chips they have available far better than they have done in the past. The Beaverbrook timber case study described earlier offers ample evidence to support this observation.

Conclusion

Guyana offers, as we have witnessed, a microcosm of so many of the challenges facing the poorer countries of the world in building a more sustainable development future. The experience it has undergone carries many lessons with it for other countries who share a similar legacy, and the tensions and dichotomies provoked by economic growth. Answers are not easy. Merely posing the challenge of sustainable development does not mean the challenge will be adequately answered. Yet posing the challenge invokes a way of thinking about problems which can try to anticipate potential pitfalls which may lie ahead and encourage appropriate preventive action.

Notes

1. EIU, *Guyana Country Report,* 4th Quarter, 1996, p.27.

2. Swedeplan, *Guyana Shorezone Management Program Design and Feasibility Study*, Swedeplan, Sweden, 1995.

3. Minewatch, "Five Minutes Before Midnight", Minewatch Briefing Document, No 24, December 1995, p.1.

4. <u>Financial</u> *Times*, 1 September 1995.

5. Minewatch, *op cit.*

6. EIU, *op cit*, 4th Quarter 1996, p.27.

7. Halcrow plc, *Draft Georgetown Water and Sewerage Master Plan*, Part IV, Vol 1, Swindon, 1994.

8. M. Pelling, "What determines vulnerability to floods: a case study in Georgetown, Guyana" in *Environment and Urbanisation*, forthcoming, 1997.

9. M. Pelling: "Household and community level hazard management options in a flood prone urban environment: Georgetown, Guyana", a paper presented at "Land, Sea and Human Effort in the Caribbean Basin" Symposium of the 28th Annual International Geographical Congress Conference, August 1996; and *Flood hazard, institutional stress and household vulnerability: coastal Guyana*, a paper given at the Conference on Environment and Development in Guyana, Centre for Developing Areas Research, Royal Holloway, University of London, 7 May 1997.

10. National Democratic Institute for International Affairs (NDIIA), *Local Democracy in Guyana. An Institutional Assessment,* NDIIA, Washington DC, 1995, p.8.

11. *ibid.*

12. *ibid*, p.12.

13.   *ibid*, p.18.

14.   L. Peake, "Living in Poverty in Linden. Guyana in the 1990s: bauxite, the "development of poverty" and household coping mechanisms" a paper for the Second Institute of British Geographers British-Caribbean Seminar, July-August 1995.

15.   K.M. Bennett, "Economic decline and the growth of the informal sector: the Guyana and Jamaica experience", *Journal of International Development*, Vol 7, No 2, 1995, pp.229-242.

16.   C.Y. Thomas, "Foreign currency black markets: lessons from Guyana", *Social and Economic Studies,* 38, 1989, pp.137-184.

17.   Bennet, *op cit*, p.237.

18.   Thomas (1989) *op cit*.

19.   Bennet, *op cit*, p.241.

20.   C. Y. Thomas, "Lessons from experience: structural adjustment and poverty in Guyana", *Social and Economic Studies*, Vol 42, 1993, p.144.

21.   J. Massiah, "Women's lives and livelihoods: a view from the Commonwealth Caribbean", *World Development*, Vol 17, No 7, 1989, p.966.

22.   *ibid*, p.968.

23.   T. Ferguson, *Structural Adjustment and Good Governance: The Case of Guyana,* Public Affairs Consulting Enterprise, Georgetown, 1995.

24.   D. Kaimowitz, "The Political Economy of Environmental Policy Reform in Latin America", *Development and Change*, Vol 27, 1996, pp.433-452.

25.   UNDP, *Guyana, Development Cooperation Report 1990* UNDP, November 1991.

26.   Kaimowitz, *op.cit*, p.438.

27.   Its first publication, *AMEG News* Vol 1, No 1, appeared in November 1996.

28.   T. Geuze and P. van den Ende, *Agroforestry in Guyana: Guidelines for Establishment and Management of Agroforestry Practices,* Inter-American Institute for Cooperation on Agriculture, Georgetown, 1996.

29.   *CAJANAR: Caribbean Journal of Agriculture and Natural Resources,* Vol 1, No 1, 1996.

30.   H. Jeffrey and R.T.L. Sang (eds), *Sustainable Development in the Guianas*, University of Guyana, Turkeyen, 1993.

31.   L. Peake, "The development and role of women's political organisations in Guyana" in J. Momsen (ed), *Women and Change in the Caribbean*, James Currey, London, 1993.

32.   L. Peake, "From social bases to subjectivities: the case of Red Thread in Guyana" in R. Keil, G. Wekerle and D. Bell (eds), *Global Cities in Local Places: Issues in Urban Sustainability*, Black Rose, Toronto.

33.   B. Munslow and F. Ekoko, "Is democracy necessary for sustainable development", *Democratization*, Vol 2, No 2, 1995.

34.   Kaimowitz, *op cit*, p.449.

Bibliography

C.L. Abernethy, *Recommendations for a Future Sea Defence Strategy,* Hydraulics Research Station, Wallingford, 1980.

An Association of village groups for Christian action in the Mazaruni river, "Letter to the Commissioner, Guyana Geology and Mines Commission", Georgetown, 20 August 1989.

M.J. Balick, "Useful plants of the Amazon", in G. Prance and T. Lovejoy (eds). *Key Environments: Amazonia,* Pergamon Press, Oxford, 1985.

K.M. Bennett, "Economic decline and the growth of the informal sector: the Guyana and Jamaica experience", *Journal of International Development,* Vol. 7, No. 2, 1995, pp 229-242.

Bureau of Statistics, *Guyana Statistical Bulletin,* Vol. 4, No. 1, Bureau of Statistics, Georgetown, 1995.

S. Cairncross, "Water supply and the urban poor", in J.E. Hardoy, S. Cairncross and D. Satterthwaite (eds), *The poor die young: Housing and Health in Third World Cities,* Earthscan, London, 1990, Chapter 5.

Caribbean Journal of Agriculture and Natural Resources, Vol. 1, Nol, 1996.

C. Caufield, *In the Rainforest,* Picador, London, 1986.

Central Housing and Planning Authority, *Government of Guyana Housing Policy,* CHPA, Georgetown, 1993.

M. Colchester and L. Lohmann, *The Tropical Forestry Action Plan: What Progress?,* World Rainforest Movement and The Ecologist, 1990.

M. Colchester, "Guyana: fragile frontier", *Race and Class,* Vol. 38, No. 4, 1997.

M. Colchester, *Guyana: fragile frontier: loggers miners and forest peoples,* Latin America Bureau, London, 1997.

A.B. Coulson, "Impact of mining developments on Amerindian communities in Interior Guyana", a paper given at the conference in Environment and Development in Guyana, Centre of Developing Areas Research, Royal Holloway, University of London, 7 May 1997.

Crewe and Warner, *A Review of Environmental Aspects of Dredge and Small Pit Mining Operations,* made in consultation with the Commonwealth Secretariat, for the Goverment of Co-operative Republic of Guyana, January 1991.

S. de Coura Cuentro and D.M. Gadji, "The collection and movement of household garbage", in J.E. Hardoy, S. Cairncross and D. Satterthwaite (eds), *The poor die young: Housing and Health in Third World Cities*, Earthscan, London 1990, Chapter 8.

A. Dalfelt, *Nature conservation survey of the Republic of Guyana*, IUCN, Mimeo, 1978.

H.G. Dalton, *The Short History of British Guyana*, Longman Brown, Green and Longmans, London, 1955.

I. Dankelman and J. Davidson (eds), *Women and Environment in the Third World*, Earthscan, London, 1988.

Dept of Mines, Western Australia, *Report on the Technological and Operational Aspects of Dredge and Small Scale Open Pit Gold and Diamond Mining in the Co-operative Republic of Guyana*, a report commissioned by the Commonwealth Secretariat, December 1990.

I. Deshmuckh, *Ecology and Tropical Biology*, Blackwell Scientific Publications, Oxford, 1986.

J. Dorst, *South America and Central America - a natural History*, Random House, New York, 1967.

The Ecologist, Vol. 25, No. 5, 1995.

Economist Intelligence Unit, *Guyana County Profile,* annual and quarterly reports, EIU, London, various years to the present.

D.B. Fanshaw, *The Vegetation of British Guyana: a preliminary review*, Institute Paper No. 29, Imperial Forest Institute, Oxford, 1952.

T. Ferguson, *Structural Adjustment and Good Governance: The Case of Guyana*, Public Affairs Consultancy Enterprise, Georgetown, 1995.

J. Forte, "Amerindians and Poverty", a paper prepared by the Amerindian Research Unit for the Institute of Development Studies seminar on Poverty, Guyana, 19 March 1993.

GAHEF Environment Unit, *Report on a site visit to Potaro River (Tumatumari Mines), 21 October 1989*, GAHEF, Georgetown, 1989.

GAHEF Environment Unit, *Report on visit to Upper Mazaruni District, 21-27 March 1990*, GAHEF, Georgetown, 1990.

GAHEF *Development Trends and Environmental Impacts in Guyana*, National Report to the United Nations Conference on Environment and Development, Rio de Janeiro, 1992.

M. Gajraj, *Development Trends and Environmental Impacts in Guyana*, a consultancy report, February 1991.

T. Geuze and P. van den Ende, *Agroforestry in Guyana: Guidelines for Establishment and Management of Agroforestry Practices*, Inter-American Institute for Cooperation on Agriculture, Georgetown, 1996.

Government of Guyana and InterAmerican Development Bank, *Urban Rehabilitation Programme. Draft report on condition of physical components*, Government of Guyana, Georgetown, 1993.

J. Gradwohl and R. Greenberg, *Saving the Tropical Forests*, Earthscan, London, 1988.

Guyana Forestry Commission and Canadian International Development Agency, *National Forestry Action Plan 1990-2000*, 1989.

Guyana Geology and Mines Commission, *Mineral Exploration Map of Guyana, Scale 1:1,000,000*, 1987.

Halcrow plc, *Draft Georgetown Water and Sewerage Master Plan*, Halcrow plc, Swindon, 1994.

M. Hanai, "Gold mining in Brazil-environmental and social impacts" in *Mining and Environment Research Network Newsletter*, No. 2, April 1992.

M. Hanif, *An overview of the natural resources of Guyana*, Institute of Applied Science and Technology, Georgetown, 1988.

S. Hecht and A. Cockburn, *The Fate of the Forest*, Penguin, London, 1990.

C. Henfrey, *The Gentle People. A journey among the Indian tribes of Guiana*, Hutchinson, London, 1964.

M.Z. Hussian, *Restoration and Expansion of the Mangrove Belt in Guyana*, a report prepared for the Hydraulics Division of the Ministry of Agriculture by FAO, Rome, May 1990.

Institute of Marine Research, *Surveys of the Fish Resources in the Shelf Areas between Surinam and Columbia 1988*, a study carried out under the NORAD/UNDP/FAO programme, Bergen, 1988.

H. Jeffrey and R.T.L. Sang (eds), *Sustainable Development in the Guianas*, University of Guyana, Turkeyen, 1993.

D. Kaimowitz, "The Political Economy of Environmental Policy Reform in Latin America", *Development and Change*, Vol. 27, 1996, pp 433-452.

V.C. Lakham, "Planning and Development Experiences in the Coastal Zone of Guyana", *Ocean and Coastal Management*, 22, 1993, pp 169-186.

R.B. Latchmansingh, "Sea Defence Construction in Guyana, Models Adopted, Difficulties Experienced", Caribbean Engineering and Management Consultants (internal document), Georgetown, 1995.

J.C. Lindemann and S.A. Mori, "The Guiannas", in D. Campbell and D. Dammond (eds), *Floristic Inventory of Tropical Countries*, New York Botanical Garden, New York, 1989.

J. Lutzenberger, "Who is destroying the Amazon Rainforest", *The Ecologist*, Vol. 17, No. 4/5, 1987, pp 155-160.

J.A. Machado, "Los hurones de la selva", in *Amazonia, la selva cercade*, El Pais, Madrid, 1990.

B. Maguire, "On the Flora of the Guyana Highfield", *Biogropica*, Vol. 2, No. 2, 1970, pp 85-100.

J. Massiah, "Women's Lives and livelihoods: a view from the Commonwealth Caribbean", *World Development*, Vol. 17, No. 7, 1989.

D. Minott, "The potential of renewable energy in the Caribbean", in M.R. Bhagavan and S. Karekezi (eds), *Energy for Rural Development*, Zed Books, London, 1992.

B. Munslow and F. Ekoko, "Is democracy necessary for sustainable development", *Democratization*, Vol.2, No. 2, 1995.

National Democratic Institute for International Affairs *Local Democracy in Guyana. An Institutional Assessment*, NDIIA, Washington DC, 1995.

A. Parasam, "Market certification of timber products from Guyana", a paper given at the conference on Environment and Development in Guyana, Centre for Developing Areas Research, Royal Holloway, University of London, 7 May 1997.

C. Pastakia, *Assessment of Institutional Capabilities in Environmental Management and Proposals for Institutional Strengthening*, a report for GAHEF under Inter-American Development Bank Technical Co-operation, December 1989.

L. Peake, "The development and role of women's political organisations in Guyana", in J. Momsen (ed.), *Women and Change in the Caribbean*, James Currey, London, 1993.

L. Peake, "Living in Poverty in Linden. Guyana in the 1990s: bauxite, the development of poverty and household coping mechanisms", a paper for the Second Institute of British Geographers British-Caribbean Seminar, July-August 1995.

L. Peake, "From co-operative socialism to a social housing policy? Declines and revivals in housing policy in Guyana", in P. Potter and D. Conway (eds), *Housing in the Caribbean*, Indiana University Press, Bloomington, 1996.

L. Peake, "From social bases to subjectivities : the case of Red thread in Guyana", in R.Keil, G. Wekerle and D. Bell (eds), *Global Cities in Local Places: Issues in Urban Sustainability*, Black Rose , Toronto, forthcoming.

D. Pearce, "Deforesting the Amazon: Toward an Economic Solution", *Ecodecision*, Vol. 1, No. 1, 1991, pp 40-48.

D. Pearce, "An Economic Approach to Saving the Tropical Forests", in D. Helm (ed), *Economic Policy Towards the Environment*, Blackwell, Oxford, 1991.

D. Pearce *et.al.*, *Blueprint2*, Earthscan, London, 1991.

M. Pelling, "Household and community level hazard management options in a flood prone urban environment: Georgetown, Guyana", a paper presented at the Land, Sea and Human Effort in the Caribbean Basin Symposium of the 28th Annual International Geographical Congress Conference, August 1996.

M. Pelling, "What determines vulnerability to floods: a case study in Georgetown Guyana", *Environment and Urbanisation*, April 1997.

M. Pelling, "Flood hazard, institutional stress and household vulnerability: coastal Guyana", a paper given at the Conference in Environment and Development in Guyana, Centre for Developing Areas Research, Royal Holloway, University of London, 7 May 1997.

D. Poore, *No Timber without Trees: Sustainability in the Tropical Forest*, Earthscan, London, 1989.

I. Rambajan, "Highly prevalent Falciparum malaria in North West Guyana: its development history and control problems", *Bulletin of PAHO*, Vol. 28, No. 3. 1994.

G. Carleton Ray, "Sustainable use of the Global Ocean", in D.B. Botkin, M.F. Caswell, J.E. Estate and A.A. Orio (eds), *Changing the Global Environment: Perspectives on Human Involvement*, Academic Press, Boston, 1989.

M. Richards, *Missing a Moving Target? Colonist Technology Development on the Amazon Frontier*, ODI, London 1997.

A. Sanders, *The Powerless People*, Macmillan, London, 1987.

R. Saunier, "Integrated Regional Development Planning, Santiago and Mira River Basins, Ecuador", in C. Conroy and M. Litvinoff (eds), *The Greening of Aid*, Earthscan, London, 1988, pp. 162-167.

G. Schuerholz, *Kaitur National Park, Guyana, Diagnostic Report*, GAHEF, Ministry of Trade and WWF, March, 1991.

C. Singh, *Guyana : Politics in a Plantation Society,* Praeger, New York, 1988.

G. Sutton, "Barama Company Project, Northwest Guyana", a paper given at the conference on Environment and Development in Guyana, Centre for Developing Areas Research, Royal Holloway, University of London, 7 May, 1997.

Swedeplan, *Guyana Shorezone Management Program Design and Feasibility Study,* Swedeplan, Sweden, 1995.

C.Y. Thomas, "Foreign currency black markets: lessons from Guyana", *Social and Economic Studies,* Vol.38, 1989, pp 137-184.

C.Y. Thomas, "Lessons from experience: structural adjustment and poverty in Guyana", *Social and Economic Studies,* Vol. 42, 1993.

C.Y. Thomas, *Social Development and the Social Summit: A look at Guyana, Jamaica and Trinidad and Tobago*, IDS, University of Guyana, Georgetown, 1995.

Tropenbos, *The Tropenbos Programme Information Series 1,* Tropenbos Foundation, 1989.

A. Trotz, "Gender, ethnicity and familial ideology in Georgetown, Guyana: Household Structure and female labour force participation reconsidered", mimeo, n.d..

UNDP, *GEF Assistance to the Programme for Sustainable Tropical Forestry Project Document*, No. GUY/91/A/99,1991.

UNDP, *Guyana, Development Cooperation Report 1990*, UNDP, Georgetown, November 1991.

L. Villegas and A. Dragovich, "The Guianas-Brazil Shrimp Industry", in J.A. Gullard and B.J. Rothschild, *Penaid Shrimp: Their Biology and Management*, U.S. Department of Commerce, Miami, 1984.

G.W. Walrond, "Exploration in Guyana", Paper No. 38 in *Proceedings of First International Symposium on Mineral Exploration Programmes*, Madrid, 1989.

A. Warhurst, *Environmental Management in Mining and Mineral Processing in Developing Countries: Enterprise Behaviour and National Policies*, Science Policy Research Unit, Sussex. 1991.

A. Warhurst, "Towards Environmental Best-Practice in Metals Production", a paper preprared for the Second Mining and Environment Research Network Workshop, Wiston House, Steyning, UK, September 1992.

E.M. Watkin and W.H. Woolford, "Alluvial Gold Mining in Guyana: Environmental Aspects", a paper presented at the Institution of Mining and Metallurgy, Minerals, Metals and the Environment Conference, Manchester 1992.

P. Williams, "Institutional framework for land management in Guyana", a paper given at the conference on Environment and Development in Guyana, Centre for Developing Areas Research, Royal Holloway, University of London, 7 May 1997.

World Bank, *Guyana: A Framework For Economic Recovery*, W.B., Washington D.C., 1985.

World Bank, *Guyana: Recent Economic Developments, Medium Term Prospects and Background to the Government's Project List 1992-9*, World Bank, Washington D.C., 24 June 1991.

World Bank, *World Development Report 1992*, WB/UNDP, Washington D.C., 1992.

World Bank, *Guyana: Public Sector Review*, W.B., Washington DC, 1993.